PR

YOU NEED PR

"Jenna Guarneri has written a must-read for all entrepreneurs needing PR for their startup. Read this book—and learn from one of the best."

—MICHAEL MCFALL, co-CEO and cofounder of
Biggby Coffee and author of *Grind*

"This book is a distillation of the wisdom and techniques Jenna used to get my startup covered by some of the biggest names in media: *The Wall Street Journal*, *The New York Times*, NPR, *The Economist*, and others. With the strategies outlined in this book, she helped me craft the story and spread the word—to great effect!"

—KATHY HANNUN, founder and president of Dandelion Energy

"PR can be a daunting undertaking for any entrepreneur, especially those who are in the hectic phase of exponential growth, and tends to fall to the end of the to-do list. Paradoxically, it's also probably the most powerful level-up tool a business builder has in their arsenal. In *You Need PR*, Jenna shares her formidable expertise and makes this crucial practice approachable and executable for every startup."

—NICOLE PORTWOOD, C-level brand builder

"In the early days of building a startup, to spend or not to spend on PR feels like a life-or-death decision. *You Need PR* takes that decision off the table for companies that need the tools—but don't have the budget—to build the foundation of a great PR strategy. Add this book to the short list of must-haves for startup founders!"

—KENDRICK NGUYEN, CEO and cofounder of Republic

"Jenna's *You Need PR* is a must-read for any business venture, especially start-ups. Following her own business-building success story, her book is personal, practical, and easily readable. Every entrepreneur should have *You Need PR* on their desk."

—HOWARD GELTZER, cofounder of Geltzer & Company and counselor with the SCORE unit of the Small Business Administration

"The analogy that 'it's a marathon, not a sprint' is so true in running a business, and nothing can help on that long-term journey more than a rock-solid PR strategy from the start. Jenna Guarneri is an expert in the field, and *You Need PR* is an amazing resource for startups to help them plan their path in how to tell their story, leverage success, and find the right partners along the journey."

—EMILY DARCHUCK, founder and CEO of Wheyward Spirit

"*You Need PR* is a comprehensive guide full of important information for startup founders and CEOs who want to begin their PR journey and don't know where to start. Jenna offers valuable expertise and advice that was tough to find until now."

—SUSAN STONE, CEO of Ubiquitous Energy

"PR is the fuel that helps early-stage startups truly take off. In *You Need PR*, Jenna Guarneri shares the strategies and tricks that she used to get UrbanStems off the launchpad—all in an easy-to-implement format that you can start right now!"

—JEFF SHEELY AND AJAY KORI, cofounders of UrbanStems

"Take a seat with this book and make moves! *You Need PR* is a fantastic guide for startups to identify and execute their strategic vision."

—DR. TIFFANY MOHR, director of PR program at
Collins College of Professional Studies, St. John's University

"Every entrepreneur needs to read *You Need PR*. What Jenna Guarneri understands is something that is highly valuable."

—DARNELL "SUPERCHEF" FERGUSON,
celebrity chef and restauranteur

YOU NEED PR

{ " An Approachable Guide
to Public Relations for
Early-Stage Companies " }

JENNA GUARNERI

AN INC.
ORIGINAL

An Inc. Original
New York, New York
www.anincoriginal.com

This work is being published under the *An Inc. Original* imprint
by an exclusive arrangement with *Inc. Magazine*. *Inc. Magazine* and
the *Inc.* logo are registered trademarks of Mansueto Ventures, LLC.
The *An Inc. Original* logo is a wholly owned trademark of Mansueto
Ventures, LLC.

Distributed by River Grove Books

Design and composition by Greenleaf Book Group and Mimi Bark
Cover design by Greenleaf Book Group and Mimi Bark
Cover images used under license from ©Shutterstock.com/
Arramdhani Design

Publisher's Cataloging-in-Publication data is available.

Print ISBN: 978-1-63909-004-4

eBook ISBN: 978-1-63909-006-8

First Edition

To my parents, Linda and William Guarneri,
and my grandparents, Jerry and Paca Scarpati

There is only one thing in life worse than
being talked about, and that is not being talked about.

—OSCAR WILDE, *The Picture of Dorian Gray*

Contents

PART IV: DELIVER

Introduction

"**I** need PR."

I often hear these three words from business owners after I tell them I run a public relations (PR) agency out of New York. I could have just met the person, and as soon as they hear what I do, their eyes light up, and they immediately open up about their business and how they are struggling to get their name out there. It's as if I've become their therapist for their brand-awareness issues. By all means, I thrive on these conversations, so feel free to stop me at a networking event or even as I'm walking down the street in NYC. But from that initial quick reaction I receive, I can tell the person never really had someone to ask these types of questions of or even a resource they could refer to for guidance.

This makes me think of when my company, JMG Public Relations, was in its infancy and I was much greener as an entrepreneur. I didn't go to business school, so my skill was in my craft as a publicist. As I grew and became wiser, I learned that being an entrepreneur wasn't just about being good at my trade; it was also about being good at human resources, accounting, marketing, and so forth. To succeed, I needed to know enough about each category to run the department efficiently—or adequately enough—myself until I had the funds to outsource it to the top professionals who did it for a living.

This is where I find early-stage entrepreneurs are with PR. They want more exposure, but they don't have the funds to hire a PR company, and what they know about PR themselves is generally minimal. So, if they attempt to do PR themselves, they can only get so far. A goal for most is to be able to hire a PR professional to take it over for them, but most PR firms require a six-month to one-year commitment consisting of a monthly retainer that's in the thousands. It's a high cost of entry for a bootstrapped or early-stage company, but the results that can come from PR can bring high value to a brand, which is a great return on the initial investment.

WHY YOU NEED PR

As an entrepreneur, you focus on innovation and on growing your brand while being conscious of your bottom line. You also look at your return on investment (ROI) and strategies that will create instantaneous results. And you focus on developing your product (or service), building a team, executing a sales strategy, and even pushing out marketing. But what always comes last on the list is the development of a PR strategy and the hiring of adequate PR professionals. The reason for this is that many times founders compare PR with marketing, and while marketing is quantifiable, PR is not, and its results really come to fruition over the long term. These results come from cultivating relationships with the media and building trust in your brand with consumers. Thus, when PR does not produce a direct sale or an instant uptick in traffic back to your website, as the founder you may prematurely assume PR is not worth the investment.

One of the biggest differences between marketing and public relations is that in marketing, a company pays for their own advertisements. In public relations, you (or a publicist) are pitching reporters to write a story about you, which requires no fee. It is a third party speaking about you and hopefully creating a positive endorsement for your brand.

In reality, PR falls more into the creative space, because it targets the subconscious through storytelling. Through the art of verbal presentation, words can paint a picture, and that picture will be unique to each and every listener. In *A Citizen's Guide to Public Relations*, Ivy Lee, known as the "father of modern public relations," said in 1928, "Publicity is the art of influencing [other people's] minds." He goes on to explain, "It is not advertising, although advertising is a part of publicity, nor is it the knack of getting desirable notices into the press. . . . Properly conceived, publicity is the sum of all the arts used to influence public opinion and move it in a desired direction."[1]

This century-old concept could not be any more relevant than it is to the businesses of today. Public relations is a long-term strategy that involves sending consistent messages through every possible communication channel that exists. PR is about influencing the perception of your audience to create an impact on their subconscious, which allows you to develop trust with the reader while simultaneously increasing your credibility as a brand.

WHAT THIS BOOK WILL DO FOR YOU

Did you know that about 90 percent of startups fail within the first five years of operation? One of the major reasons a startup fails is poor marketing, which includes the brand awareness developed through strategic PR strategies. Having the right exposure is vital to securing new clients, company growth, future funding, and your company's success. In *You Need PR*, I share with you the tools that will allow any startup to manage their own PR initiatives and be successful in their efforts.

You may be asking yourself if you fall into the spectrum of a startup. Keep in mind, a startup is not just a newly established company. Your company could be considered a startup even if it has been around more than five years and has thirty-plus employees. The word *startup* simply means any company that has the ability to scale, has an innovation designed to solve a problem, or makes the lives of its end users easier.

WHAT TO EXPECT IN THE PAGES AHEAD

You Need PR was written by a founder for founders. We are our clients. We as a PR firm are a startup. We understand what it takes to get noticed, and we know how to use what you have to secure press even with an evergreen story angle. We understand every dollar counts and that paid media isn't ideal, so we want to help other founders like you understand PR in a way that will help you secure earned media coverage for yourself and your startup.

This book is divided into four parts. Part I discusses how to *establish* yourself as a brand and what you need to do first to lay the foundation for a successful PR campaign. PR is important to the long-term success of a startup, because it considers all the factors that go into building a loyal following. *You Need PR* is designed to teach you how to look at your startup from a more holistic perspective, analyzing every possible channel that a message can be delivered through. It allows you to look through the lens of your audience and how they perceive you during each and every touchpoint. It also talks about the "human perspective" and why it's important to humanize your interactions during the PR process, as well as why it's important to continuously develop content.

Part II helps you *build* your press materials and develop the best possible story. It also addresses knowing your competitor landscape and how your competitors are delivering their messages, as well as how the media is speaking about them.

Part III helps you formulate a strategy before you *launch* your PR initiatives. It also covers what you need to know about the media before engaging with them. Then, once you have the foundation laid, the materials built, and the knowledge for properly managing the process, you will be ready to draft and execute on the pitching process.

Part IV covers how to *deliver* on the media interview. It discusses the best methods for following up with your pitches and offers examples of possible responses you may receive from reporters. It discusses how to manage an interview and provides actual interview tips. It also reviews what to do after the media hit runs.

While the world was going through so many changes during the onset of the COVID-19 pandemic, I decided from the moment of shutdown to use the extra time I was given at home to chronicle all the tools and ideas a company or an individual needs to implement a successful public relations strategy. Am I giving away the secret sauce? Maybe, but when a company gets to the point where they can hire the PR firm to do the work for them, they always do, because it's one less thing they have to do. Until you get to that point, I suggest you grab some coffee, settle into a cozy nook, and prepare to learn the PR process, start to finish. When you're ready, turn the page, and let's get started.

{ Part I }

ESTABLISH

CHAPTER 1

Laying the Foundation

Whatever you can do, or dream you can do, begin it.
Boldness has genius, power, and magic in it!

—W. H. MURRAY, *The Scottish Himalayan Expedition*

We all want to be successful. That's why we start a business in the first place. We want to create something that will impact others and that people rely on so much they keep coming back for more. We start a business with such zest and excitement that we expect everyone else to be just as eager as we are. But in reality, when the doors open and the sales aren't pouring in, what good can our company do if no one knows we exist?

A well-recognized brand can achieve many things, including an increase in sales or user signups; an increase in traffic back to the website, which, in turn, will increase your search engine optimization; an increase in funding from investors; and an increase in leadership and authority within your own space. If you are the first of your kind, you do not want a competitor claiming they were first, just because they started to talk about it in the media before you did. By securing media coverage, you are putting on record your story and ownership.

Brand recognition is the ability of consumers to recall your brand. Can successful companies really exist without proper brand recognition? Probably not. This doesn't mean that you have to be a household name; not every company will be a business-to-consumer (B2C) business model, which is what you need to be in order to be that well recognized. If you are a business-to-business (B2B) model, then it is recognition and notoriety within your niche category that you will want to achieve.

Public relations (PR) requires you to put yourself out there in ways that may not be very comfortable for you. At times, it can require you to be the loudest person in the room. *Merriam-Webster* defines *public relations* as "the business of inducing the public to have understanding for and goodwill toward a person, firm, or institution."[1] PR is all about perception. It's about the messages you are distributing through each and every communication channel and the stories you are telling that represent who you are as a brand. The more people you tell about it, the more people will talk about it.

The Small Business Association estimates that there are over 627,000 new businesses that open each year.[2] In today's growing world, the competition is increasing, and offering something new and innovative will be key to your competitive edge and a top-line talking point when promoting the brand. It is no longer enough to offer a great product or service; it needs to be distinctively different, with a feature that consumers can't find elsewhere. This innovation will be the starting point toward laying the groundwork for an effective PR campaign.

PR IS ABOUT PERCEPTION

When a new house is constructed, the builder pulls together the brightest professionals from each construction trade. It takes twenty-two subcontractors to build the average home. Specialists are needed to build out the foundation and others to work on framing, plumbing, electric, flooring, drywall, masonry, HVAC, and so forth. Each trade cannot start their work until another starts or finishes theirs. The drywall cannot start until the electrical wires are installed, for example, and the electric can't be started until the framing is done. It's an interconnected system that relies on the success of each part in order to function properly. One faulty wire and you run the risk of the whole system burning.

Public relations has a similar interconnected system, which I call the theory of the *constructed perception*. In construction, the beautiful final product is the move-in-ready home, and in PR, the final product is the perception ready to be received by your audience. Like the construction of a home, the perception is built through strategic tasks that are properly executed and reliant on one another in order to build a sustainable and robust ecosystem.

The rooms of the home resemble the different messages being issued, and the nuts and bolts represent the series of factors you consider when crafting your message. The foundation of the home represents who you are as a brand, why you exist, and the innovation you provide. If your startup is not clear about who you are up front, then your audience will never understand what you are trying to convey. Your messages will never be clear, and you'll never have the opportunity to connect with your audience.

How an individual perceives you will affect whether they decide to support you. Public relations isn't just about a feature story in a media outlet; it's about the perception of the writer, consumer, investor, and anyone who comes in contact with your brand. It's about the way a customer service representative treats a current or potential customer; that behavior and that engagement relate directly back to the overall image and credibility of the startup. If someone has a bad interaction with a representative from your startup, your image as a startup is in jeopardy. A bad review spreads faster than a wildfire via word of mouth.

Zendesk reports that 54 percent of customers share bad experiences with more than five people, while only 33 percent share their good experiences.[3] A customer who was emotionally triggered has the conviction inside them to say something and maybe even do something about their bad interaction. If a customer was given a good experience, they might not be triggered enough to have a reaction. The negative customer experiences can be the most detrimental to your business and are harder to control after they happen. It's better to be proactive in the prevention of those instances by ensuring that you and your team understand perception and the value it brings to the business.

Perception refers to the set of processes someone takes when interpreting and forming an opinion on a person or given subject matter. *Direct perception* is based on in-person encounters, where the person is standing in front of you and is able to chat with you and see your nonverbal cues. There are no outside influences; their perception is based on their own personal experience. *Mediated perception* is based on secondhand interactions. For instance, if someone is reading about you in a newspaper, they are reading about you through the eyes of the writer. Your intended message can be skewed by the writer, who has their own bias and interpretation of the message that you gave them. Then you have the reader to consider. They will be reading the text that the writer wrote on your behalf and will insert their own experiences and biases into the written text. And what they perceive from that writing will depend on their own personal understanding. PR is a precautionary method that preserves the way you want to be perceived by both the direct and the mediated audience, ensuring your message delivery aligns with you and your startup.

Every word issued by your company counts. It only takes a handful of words to create an unforgettable moment. Take, for instance, the massive BP oil spill in the Gulf of Mexico in 2010, which was the largest in the history of marine oil-drilling operations. The Center for Biological Diversity reported 205.8 million gallons of oil and 225,000 tons of methane were released into the water. Eleven people perished and 82,000 birds of 102 different species were harmed or killed, along with approximately 6,165 sea turtles, 25,900 marine mammals, and a vast number of fish.[4]

The day after the spill, CEO Tony Hayward stated to several media outlets, "I'd like my life back."[5] Those five words gave the perception of Hayward as a selfish individual who had complete disregard for the magnitude of the disaster his company created, not just for the world's ecosystem but for the immediate families of those eleven people who were killed. From the perspective of a PR specialist, it is unlikely that Hayward had his words reviewed by a PR team; if he had, they would have ensured his personal words aligned with the values of BP, which would have exemplified more compassion toward those affected.

Stages of Perception

Perception is how people process and interpret the information around them. There are five stages of perception: stimulation, organization, interpretation-evaluation, memory, and recall.

Stimulation

Perception begins with the senses: sight, smell, hearing, taste, and touch. For stimulation to occur, sensory receptors need to send signals that will stimulate the brain. Someone must first sense something before they can perceive it. Without a stimulus being sent to their brain, they will not be able to continue on to the other stages.

The first phase of perception is key to a public relations strategy. It is your first touchpoint with your audience and where you will need to have the most impact on them in order for the other stages of perception to occur. Think of someone walking into a bookstore looking for their next book to read while on vacation. They aren't sure just yet what they want, but they figure they'll walk through and see if something catches their eye. If a book looks like every other book on the shelf, they will be less inclined to pick it up. But if a book is unique in its jacket design and has a catchy title, their brain will receive the stimuli for further engagement.

Organization

The world as we know it is filled with noise and clutter. Because of this, a person's brain cannot focus on all the stimuli presented to them. What they notice is based on environmental factors and their own personal experiences. This is why it's important to deliver messages continuously. Not every message will get through. Once received, the information from the stimuli gets sent to the brain for organization into a meaningful pattern. To better make sense of the new information, the brain attempts to draw comparisons between the new information and the information the brain has stored from past experiences.

When creating your PR strategy, you'll want to find messaging that will address the pain points of your audience to increase the likelihood of the new information relating back to the stored information in their memory. Pain points relate to a problem someone is facing that is troubling or even a nuisance to their everyday life.

Interpretation-Evaluation

The interpretation step, according to Joseph A. DeVito, is when an individual evaluates the stimulus. This evaluation is greatly influenced by the person's experiences, needs, wants, values, beliefs about the way things are or should be, expectations, physical and emotional state, and so on.[6] It is also influenced by their rules, scripts, and gender. For example, an individual who meets someone new who has the same profession as their father once had will be able to relate to and understand that person better, as opposed to someone who meets a new person and doesn't know anything about their profession.

Memory

The stimuli may even generate fond memories and create an emotional connection. Within your PR strategy, you'll want your messaging to properly portray the values and wants of your audience so they can appropriately interpret the common relation between them and your startup. The memory stage is marked by the storage of information to long- and short-term memory. In time, something will jog the memory, and the mind will try to recall what it already knew and heard about the stimulus.

Recall

With every PR campaign, you'll want your message or stimuli to be impactful and meaningful enough to create a memory that is positively recalled. If your product offers joy or excitement, your customer will be more likely to remember it. Positive associations create stronger brand memories, and positive brand associations will create an increase in sales.

Empathy: The Art of Treating Others with Compassion

What you learned as a child continues to be a lesson taught in business: It's important to be nice to people. Empathy takes patience, and it's something we often lose sight of because we are caught up in the startup life. There are times you have to take on the work of a few different roles, and then there are times you have to continuously change your work to keep up with the changes that happen so quickly in a startup. You're busy, and it's easy to forget to take a moment to connect and make deep, meaningful connections with people. Realistically, though, your startup cannot survive if you aren't making your customers feel heard and understood. "While you have to act within the boundaries of what your brand stands for, empathy is the most important thing: Your employees should meet your customers where they are, and treat them as people," said Seth Godin, business executive and author of nineteen best-selling books, including *Purple Cow* and *Linchpin*.[7] By doing so, you stand out from your competitors and show that you not only have a great product or service to sell but also care about the people purchasing it.

How in your public relations strategy do you create this human effect? How do you connect with your audience on a deeper level to create an emotional, positive connection? The answer is through meaningful and valuable content driven by empathy. Treating your audience with compassion shows that you are not viewing their interaction as just a transaction or even a sale. You are demonstrating how you as a brand care about them as individuals and want to build long-term relationships with them. You are shaping their long-term perception of your startup from early on.

DEFINING YOUR PURPOSE

Before you shout out to the world that you're here and ready to do business, you need to have a clear understanding of what you want your brand to represent. By better understanding who you are as a startup, you will be better able to determine the messages you want issued and how you want them to be perceived.

Brand Identity: Understanding Your "Who"

It's important to have a clear vision of the goals of your business, the innovation you are offering, and your overall brand identity. To make an emotional connection with your audience, you first need to understand who your audience is. Who you are will often be defined by what your competitors lack. The competitive edge is an important point to weave into messaging; audiences will then recognize the innovation without it having to be told directly. Likely, if you are calling yourselves "innovators," no one will believe you. Rather, it's important for your audience to come to this determination on their own by hearing the innovation. Allow those competitor differences to sell themselves and attract the clients that need what you offer.

Your business goals are defined by what you want to accomplish in your work. When deciding what your goals are, be as specific as possible. By having a clear vision, you will be better positioned to create profitability, growth, and impact. Looking at your startup over both the long term and short term will help you create actionable tasks that will support you in reaching each of your benchmarks. Within your goals, you'll want to break down the demographics of your core customer. You can then determine in your PR strategy how you will reach those people and grab enough of their attention so they will engage with your startup.

Your brand identity is different from your overall brand image or what is similarly known as the *perceived perception*. Brand identity relates to the visual components of your startup: logos, color, typography, imagery, and so on. The visuals of your startup create a nonverbal touchpoint for your audience and are sometimes the very first impression someone will receive. If the colors are too jarring and the font too busy—or they are the complete opposite and come across as boring—you'll lose your audience. It is a delicate balance, but your goal should always be for people with varying perspectives to see and acknowledge the message. This, in turn, will lead them to engage with your startup.

Self-reflection is key when determining who you are as a brand. The idea of reality versus expectation pertains to the notion that how you think you are being perceived isn't always the reality of the perception. While you want the recipient to have a specific takeaway, they may have an entirely different takeaway than you intended. Before you communicate your message, ask yourself, "How could this message be received?" Is there anything ambiguous in your message that could be confusing or perceived in a negative way? Evaluate and consider the varying messages that can be received before sharing the information.

Who you are as a brand should be consistently relayed in your messaging and across all communication channels. The famous Marketing Rule of 7, developed by Dr. Jeffrey Lant, is one of the oldest marketing theories around. Lant states that to penetrate the buyer's consciousness and make significant penetration in a given market, you have to contact the prospect a minimum of seven times within an eighteen-month period.[8] The theory was introduced prior to cable TV, and the world has since become even more cluttered, thanks to the creation of social media. Platforms like Instagram, Twitter, Facebook, and TikTok allow everyday people to create personalized content for the entire world to see. As a result, industry professionals now have to cut through the noise from both their competitors and from everyday people.

Noise refers to the excessive amount of information available in the world, making it difficult for individuals to pick out specific messages to stimulate the brain for perception. Social media has saturated the market, creating endless content of shorter length. Our minds are overwhelmed with options, and it makes it harder for information to stand out enough to become the stimulus our minds respond to. The mindless scrolling reduces attention spans, causing industry professionals to adapt their strategies so that their startup's content is of similar size and more easily digestible. The startup community flourished in the 2000s after the dot-com boom. Since then, there has been an influx of venture capital for startups, which means there are more budgets available for public relations. The increase of public relations strategies means a rise in the amount of stories being pitched to media people. The noise continues to get louder and more cluttered, which is why more than just seven touchpoints are required to get someone's attention in today's modern world.

Core Values: Understanding Your "What"

The fundamental beliefs of your startup, also known as your *core values*, are the foundation from which you operate. They not only guide your team in their day-to-day work but also serve as the vision for all future goals. Using your core values as part of your PR strategy will help your customer understand the intrinsic purpose of your brand, and provide deeper, more meaningful content rather than the typical surface-level sales information. The core values will help you understand how you want to be perceived by others.

What are things you want people to walk away knowing and reiterating to their friends? Is it that you are a consumer-packaged-goods brand that values the donation of time and work by your employees in a less fortunate country? Or perhaps you are a pesticide startup that, surprisingly enough, strongly values sustainability. The more unique your core values are, the more it will add to your level of innovation. Innovation is not just about the design and product offering; it also relates to your business model and how you operate. The core values should be incorporated into your brand's messaging to ensure people are aware of them. To do so, first build out a list of your startup's core values.

These core values are based on your mission statement and are translated into the behaviors of each employee. The mission statement explains *why*, while your core values explain *how*. They create structure for a better and stronger team and are a shared commitment from the business and everyone in it. The core values define the company's internal messaging, which should be cohesive, inspiring, and embedded into everything you do. These core values will also be important to your startup's recruiting and employee retention, as they will naturally align with the personal values of your employees. If they do not, then the employee will be recognizable as a poor fit for your startup culture.

At JMG Public Relations, we focus our core values around three pillars: our employees, our clients, and the media. Those are the most important categories for people we engage with on any given day. To best serve each, we focus on hustling, creating, leading, and being both authentic and results driven.

By being hustlers, we make a commitment to our clients to provide them with the best services and support at all times. By being creators, we make it a priority for our employees to feel creatively stimulated in their work, for our clients to receive out-of-the-box-thinking ideas, and for the media to be offered an innovative approach to cover as their next big story. By being team leaders, we make our team's needs a priority, ensuring they are given the guidance and means to execute their tasks properly and effectively. Through authentic behaviors, we make a commitment to build genuine relationships with our media contacts, clients, and employees. And in terms of being results driven, results are key for any client-service business, so we need to continuously produce. With all the behaviors combined, we will produce results that will please our clients.

Readiness: Knowing Your "When"

When it comes to PR campaigns, you can start one anytime. It all hinges on you. Some startups are ready sooner than others. The most important point to remember is your company must be the best version of itself, otherwise any PR strategy put into place will work against you, not for you. While we all want to hit the ground running, it's important to be strategic in your planning and 100 percent clear in your brand identity; anything less than that and you will wind up with mixed messaging in the media. You don't want someone seeing your brand somewhere and being told you do one thing and then seeing it elsewhere and being told you do something else. The consumer will not stop to figure out what you mean, so you'll lose their interest without there being a clear and uniform message across all communication channels.

66 Innovation Station 99

We all know the analogy "It's a marathon, not a sprint," but aside from the obvious difference in time that requires a buildup of strength, why exactly is that important, and how does it relate to PR? Sprinting or short-distance running requires short, quick bursts of speed. Sprint work can help build muscle and increase your metabolism to help you push through your long-distance runs. But because sprinting requires your body to move at its highest intensity, it can actually cause an increase in injuries because of its explosive nature. To be prepared for your sprint, you need to work on your dynamic stretches, trial ramp-up runs, and proper technique.

The same can be said for PR. The small sprints can help in tandem with your long-term strategy, but if you do not carefully prep for those sprints, the outcome can hurt you more than help you. You can start the PR process by asking yourself, "What is unique about my startup, and what is the innovation we are offering that no one else is?" Then, "What are the core values that keep us focused as a team on our day-to-day and future goals?" Finally, "What top-line information do we want to share most with our customers so they gain a certain perception about us?"

CHAPTER 2

Getting to the Core

In this ever-changing society, the most powerful and
enduring brands are built from the heart.

—HOWARD SCHULTZ, *Pour Your Heart into It*

A customer's perception of a brand's behavior as being honest, transparent, and trustworthy is what is referred to as *brand authenticity*. It's genuine and real behavior. It's about sticking to the promises you make and seeing to it that you are presenting realistic information and not just information you think the customer wants to hear, or what I often refer to as "fluff." Genuine behaviors lay the foundation for building stronger and more meaningful connections. A report by Label Insight found that 94 percent of customers are likely to show loyalty to a brand that offers complete transparency, while 56 percent claim that brand transparency would make them "loyal for life."[1] We are inspired by these transparent brands, and because of that, we are emotionally connected to them. We may even still buy their products when there is a less expensive alternative available.

Outdoor clothing company Patagonia's core values—"build the best product," "cause no unnecessary harm," and "use business to protect nature"—are fulfilled by their investment in renewable energy.[2] They also developed the Chemical and Environmental Impacts Program to manage chemical and environmental impacts of their global supply chain and are actively campaigning for environmental causes, such as preserving America's national parks. On top of this, Patagonia is known for asking their customers to re-wear and to think twice before buying their products. In 2011, when the country was still recovering from the Great Recession that started in 2008, Patagonia released an advertisement on Thanksgiving that read, "Don't Buy This Jacket." It talked about the jacket's environmental impact, asked consumers to reconsider before buying it, and suggested they instead opt for a used Patagonia product. The result? The company's revenue grew approximately 30 percent to $543 million in 2012, followed by another 5 percent growth in 2013.[3] The unparalleled loyalty from a Patagonia customer is due to the success of their branding and their ability to continuously communicate and fulfill their brand promises.

GETTING TO KNOW YOUR BRAND

Brand loyalty is the positive feeling a customer has toward a brand that leads to their continuously choosing that brand over a competitor's.

It is the ultimate goal when building a fan base, because it means you've gained the customer's unconditional trust and support. To get to this level with a customer, you have to continuously provide them with a quality product or service they know they can rely on each time they come back to you. Brand loyalty means the customer understands you completely and is sold on your brand identity.

For a customer to be clear on who you are, you'll need to first have a clear understanding of who you are as a brand. Your communication will be about convincing others of what you already know: that you are a brand worth trying and regularly supporting. To get to this point, you'll need to drill down to the core of your company and ask yourself the important "why" and "who" questions.

Digging Deeper: Develop Your "Why"

It's the "why" that will connect your customers on an emotional level to your brand. To develop your "why," ask yourself:

- Why did I start this company?
- Why is the company important to people?
- Why should people become customers?

The brilliant Simon Sinek, author of *Start with Why: How Great Leaders Inspire Everyone to Take Action*, explains that "why" is probably the most important message that an organization or individual can communicate, as this is what inspires others to action. In Sinek's companion book, *Find Your Why*, he says, "When we align emotionally with our customers and clients, our connection is much stronger and more meaningful than any affiliation based on features and benefits."[4] Once you know your deep-rooted "whys," you can make more strategic choices for your business moving forward.

Understanding your "why" will also help you develop a clear purpose for your business, which can then be clearly communicated to your customer. To explore your "why," simply put the word *why* in front of any statement to find the deep-rooted explanation behind it. This sets the tone for a clear strategy with clear goals and expectations that align with your "why." Doing this helps customers relate to your "whys," which means you are connecting with them on a deeper level. This approach can increase trust and credibility, and that, in turn, will create increased sales and a loyal community of customers.

Key Differentiators: Know Your Competitors

Not only does knowing your "why" drive your communications strategy; it also creates a clear distinction between you and your competitors. Companies can exist by selling the same product or service, but what sets them apart is how they sell it. Even if you think you offer the best product or that it's the first of its kind, there will always be someone else offering something even fractionally similar or who has a better communication strategy than you. If they are louder and can capture the loyalty of a greater market share, customers will opt for that company over yours. So you'll want to ensure that you have a consistent strategy that will allow you to be a part of the same industry-specific conversations in the media as your competitors, help you capture the greatest market share, and put you at the forefront of all media coverage.

While onboarding new clients, we develop an in-depth competitor analysis to determine how best to position the client in the media and the key message points we need to focus on. We look at the direct competitors who offer nearly the same product or service, as well as the indirect competitors who offer a different product altogether but are seen as an alternative option for purchase. We look at how they are all positioning themselves on their website, on social media, and in the news. We also look to see what kind of press they've gotten over the last twelve months, the media outlets that have covered them, the topics of the articles they're featured in, and the key takeaways about the company within those stories. This also helps us lay the foundation for the ideal PR strategy for our clients, since it gives us a better understanding of which media outlets may cover our client and which reporters are writing about the topics most relevant to us.

After analyzing a company's competitors, we develop all the necessary materials to present to the media for review. In doing so, we answer the simple question of "What is this company doing to solve a customer's pain point?" The *pain point* refers to the problem or issue a customer is dealing with right now, will deal with in the future, or doesn't yet know is a pain point even though they are experiencing it. Addressing the pain point addresses an emotion. This, in turn, creates a human connection. This humanization allows you to get to know your customers. Once you determine your customers' pain points, compare your solution to your competitors'. How can you offer something better that will make someone want to make the switch over to you? Understanding your customers' wants and needs and how they are not being fully met by other companies will allow you to position yourself ahead of others.

THE HUMAN FACTOR

Consumers have gotten used to brands vying for their attention. The amount of competition in the market and the need to attract new business cause brands to promote overzealous sales pitches with not-so-natural, sometimes forceful messaging. This lack of personalization causes a disconnect to form between consumers and the brand.

Consumers lose trust in brands because they feel the brands are more focused on gaining another sale than on the impact their product or service will actually have on their individual consumers. A 2018 PwC survey found that 75 percent of consumers around the world desire more human interaction, while 65 percent of US consumers find a positive customer experience to be more influential than advertising.[5]

If you're a small business, you have an advantage, because chances are you're on the ground, interacting with your customers in the day-to-day business. But as your startup grows and spreads to more locations with more employees and more customers, it becomes increasingly hard to create a personalized customer experience that provides a compelling reason for the customer to support you.

FedEx Cares

For example, the shipping conglomerate FedEx has millions of packages being shipped each day from thousands of locations with hundreds of thousands of employees. It's very hard to create a personalized customer experience. To connect with people in a more meaningful way, FedEx launched FedEx Cares, which is a global community-engagement program designed to help make the world a better place through in-kind shipping, volunteering time and expertise, and charitable giving. They deliver funds, volunteers, and resources where they are needed most, especially in times of disaster. The people and causes they donate to aren't necessarily customers or even cases related to their core work as a shipping company; however, by creating this initiative, FedEx is showing their value to the places they ship to and the people who are shipping. In turn, they are creating a personalized connection with the people in those communities.

To take it one step further, the company has also pledged to help fifty million people by their fiftieth anniversary, which is documented on social media through the use of the hashtag #fedexcares. For instance, FedEx collaborated with Team Rubicon in Houston to volunteer in the rebuilding of homes impacted by Hurricane Harvey. FedEx also donated one hundred car seats to the country of Moldova, which had a high increase of road crashes involving children in 2018. FedEx's mission to support people—and their belief "that a connected world is a better world," which guides everything they do—is respected and valued by their customers.

Humanization: Treating Others with Kindness

FedEx Cares is an example of a large-scale effort, but the takeaway is similar to what we learned when we were little: It's important to acknowledge the feelings of the people you interact with while simultaneously addressing their wants and needs. This kindness or humanization builds relationships, and you can go as big or as small as you like with your efforts. Humanization creates a positive perception for current and future customers, so no effort will go lost or unnoticed.

There's the old-school method of celebrating your customers on special days like their birthdays. Think of all the people who have left restaurants with a good memory because the staff sang "Happy Birthday" to them. The goal is to have customers feel they are appreciated. No-cost methods include sending a welcome or thank-you email to customers, showing emotions through humor and real-story shares in content creation, and engaging with customers in real time who comment or share a review with you. You and your team can even volunteer in your local community and invite your customers to join in. You can also create personal connections between your staff and your customers.

One way to create personal connections is to highlight employees on social media and in-store, if applicable, by showing off their hobbies and interests. At JMGPR, for any new staff member, we share an official welcome message via Instagram and Facebook highlighting three unique facts about that person. We encourage staff to show off their quirky selves and to pick things that we may not necessarily know about them in the office. The goal with this is twofold: It encourages employees to embrace their individualism, and for those customers reading the information, they feel as if they get to know these people on a personal level. We've had people share things like they knit with their grandma on weekends, they took first place in the Miss Congeniality category during a beauty pageant, they co-own an escape room, or their family has three pet ducks.

As your business grows, so can the scale of your humanized customer-experience efforts. Large-scale efforts may require a budget. So, yes, it will cut into your bottom line, but it will create a long-term impact on your customers that will turn into a loyal brand following and repeat customers. Customers appreciate kind gestures, because these gestures show you are trying to create an emotional connection with them. This makes the consumer feel that you genuinely care about them becoming (or continuing to be) a customer of yours and aren't just looking to make one more sale.

Appreciation: Showing You Care

Whether it be toward your employees or your customers, you can never show too much appreciation. According to data collected by the US Small Business Administration, 68 percent of clients leave because they feel the company doesn't care about them.[6] In other words, customers who feel appreciated are much more likely to become repeat customers. These positive feelings will then create a direct, positive perception of your company.

Client Relations

When a new client signs on with us, we want them to have the best possible first impression, so we send a personalized gift to each of the people we will be working with. It will be the same gift for each member of the team, but it sends a personalized message. For instance, for a company that was located in Brooklyn, we found a company that created baskets using only made-in-Brooklyn products. The gift was something they likely never received before, and yes, it would have been much easier to send a generic gift, but it showed that we took a moment to care about their identity of being a Brooklyn brand themselves.

Customers love rewards. T-Mobile launched T-Mobile Tuesdays as a loyalty program that would give customers prizes from some of their favorite brands each week. The goal was not only to excite people but also to thank them for being loyal customers. No other phone company was doing something like this, and because the cell phone industry has a reputation for having unhappy customers, the action positioned T-Mobile well among phone users and really demonstrated the company's effort to create a unique, humanized connection with its customers. According to the Mobile Marketing Association, T-Mobile measured its success through three different categories: customer happiness, customer engagement, and business impact. Since the program launched in June 2016, more than eighty million customers have participated in T-Mobile Tuesdays, and the campaign has generated fifteen million downloads and forty-one million prize redemptions. Since the launch of this loyalty program, T-Mobile has seen an increase in customer satisfaction and an increase in the likelihood of its customers to both continue with and recommend its services.[7]

Employee Relations

A company with strong employee relations will see an increase in productivity and, in turn, something we all love: revenue. Gallup reported that employees who are engaged are 27 percent more likely to report "excellent" performance.[8] More so, happy employees will not only be more efficient in their work but also turn into a collective of your own brand ambassadors. Referrals are the best source of business, and your employees are a network of potential new business leads. If they love where they work and believe in the company's values, they will tell their friends about it, and consequently, their friends will be intrigued to find out more. The positive perception of the employee is then transferred to outside sources.

A simple way to find out what kind of incentives work best for your employees is to ask them in a survey. For us, it was unlimited sick days, which benefited employees in the long term, and complimentary spa days twice a year, which helped them in the short term. Other ideas we received on the survey included creating a staff appreciation day, having a break room worth the break, and supporting costs associated with commuting or daycare. Some others wanted us to create awesome company swag. To address this, we created an online "JMGPR Swag Store" just for our employees. Now they can purchase unique items our designer handcrafted for our team.

Employee incentives don't have to be at a cost to the company either. You can show your appreciation to employees in a public way by sharing an award or recognition they earned via your blog, on social media, or in-store. You can also personalize the interaction between junior and senior members of the team by creating a program that encourages them to go out to lunch together.

Transparency: Sharing Your Story

A recent study by Gallup showed that more than two-thirds of the decisions that customers make are based on emotional factors.[9] Customers are people who have basic needs. They appreciate transparency, engage with relatability, and interact with the remarkable. Let's take a step back for a second and look through the lens from an outsider's perspective. If you go to your website or social media accounts, or you look at any company-generated content, does it all feel (too) promotional? Does it sound as though you are solely trying to sell a product or service? If so, then it's time to add in more relatable content, and the best place to start is with you and your story. How and why did you start this company? Did you overcome an obstacle to get where you are today? Are you a female leader in a male-dominated industry? One of the ways you can humanize your brand is to simply embrace who you are and your background. For example, do you have a David and Goliath story? It's stories like these that are genuine and filled with honest information that customers both appreciate and value.

Warby Parker is known not only for being an alternative to the high-price eyewear industry but also for its founders' story, in which they saw a problem and wanted to produce a solution. On their website, they discuss how every idea starts with a problem and theirs was simple: Glasses are too expensive. As students, one of the founders lost his eyeglasses while on a backpacking trip, but because they were too expensive to replace, he wound up spending the first semester of grad school without them. They realized this was a common problem because the eyewear industry is "dominated by a single company that has been able to keep prices artificially high while reaping huge profits from consumers who have no other options."[10]

The Warby Parker brand identity is based on a pain point experienced by the founders themselves. That very pain point happens to be shared by millions of other people who have experienced the high prices associated with eye care. Through this relatable story, Warby Parker was able to create a community of loyal brand enthusiasts.

Engagement: Interact with Your Customer

By acknowledging the human factor in your audience, you automatically stand out from your competitors, because you are showing you not only have a great product or service to sell but also care about the people who buy it. Consumers want to purchase from brands that care about them, and social media allows companies to connect with customers in an even more personal and individualized way. Companies can respond directly to customers' comments and direct messages and even share customer-generated content, or what is better known as *user-generated content* (UGC).

People get excited when they get a social media shout-out from their favorite brand. Stackla reports that 51 percent of consumers say they'd be more likely to engage with or purchase from a brand if it shared their photo, video, or social post across its marketing channels. Interestingly enough, 45 percent of people will unfollow a brand if it does too much self-promotion.[11]

Airbnb has become well known for optimizing their UGC, as the majority of their social media content is about sharing the experiences their customers have from around the world. User photos are like testimonials, so sharing them shows a level of authenticity, which helps add to your brand's credibility while reassuring future customers who want to use your service.

Another company that utilizes UGC well is GoPro. GoPro's online campaign encourages users to post their photos using the hashtag #GoPro. By doing this, the users are demonstrating how the product works while showing how much fun they are having in their activities. This creates a case of FOMO (fear of missing out) and increases conversions, which, in turn, generates more sales.

Another method for user interaction is conversation based. Supermarket giant Whole Foods, known for their natural and organic food offerings, has become well known for their highly engaged strategy on Twitter. According to *The Wall Street Journal*, the Whole Foods global online community manager "spends about 90% of his time talking to individual shoppers."[12] Customer questions are acknowledged and responded to almost immediately, which makes the customers feel heard and respected.

Whole Foods also hosts weekly Twitter chats that prompt questions from followers and encourage them to share their own recipes or pictures with their online community. Whole Foods started to see an influx of questions pertaining to specific regional stores. To address customer needs on a local level, Whole Foods created over 250 accounts for specific communities. For instance, the Fairfax branch of Los Angeles's Tweets can be found under @WholeFoods3rdSt.

66 Innovation Station 99

When you develop your company, you're excited about the concept and think everyone will share in your excitement. While you are in development, it's important to take a step back to understand the meaning behind what you are doing and how it relates to your core customer. A good way to do this is to ask yourself, "Am

I understanding my customer in a way that no other company has done before? And am I staying true to my mission and core values?"

You can only answer these questions once you've established who your company is, which includes knowing who your company isn't. This comes from evaluating your brand on a deeper level. Communication is key to a successful business strategy, and you can't have a cohesive brand message without having a clear foundation first. So take the time to connect with both your customers and employees on a more human level. Get to know their basic wants and needs, and then communicate how your product or service can meet those. Use your personal story as a way to create a personal connection with each customer.

CHAPTER 3

Constant Content

Content is king.

—**BILL GATES,** "Content Is King"

Public relations requires that you have a strategy that consists of a constant flow of communication. This applies to even JMGPR, a PR agency ourselves! Separate from our day-to-day work with clients, we have meetings to discuss our own content strategy. For instance, we have a heavy focus on biweekly blog writing, which targets potential startup clients, and Instagram, which targets college students interested in public relations and potential internships with JMGPR. The world of PR is competitive, and content helps us appear in more search engines as well as increases the likelihood of someone organically coming across us.

The world as we know it today is filled with noise, and because your business is competing with so many different noise makers, it will be increasingly difficult for your message to be received by your target audience. By continuously developing and issuing new content, you are increasing the likelihood of your audience seeing, digesting, and engaging with a message. You are also laying the foundation to grow your audience by creating relevant and engaging content that people come to rely on, communicate to others about, and genuinely look forward to receiving. Additionally, by continuously developing content on a specific topic, you are establishing yourself as a leader in your respective field, which will further aid in your company's growth and development.

Content helps you be a part of the conversation. It's like going to a party in a room filled with hundreds of people. You know no one, until you decide to spark up a conversation with a small group hanging out next to the buffet. An open dialogue will help determine your commonality with these people. The more interesting the topics, the more likely the group will engage in the conversation, and the more likely they will be to form a bond with you. The same can be said for public relations. You as a business are showing up to the party with a goal: You want to build new relationships but need to shout over the music for people to hear you.

The type of content that works best varies from business to business. It's about finding your sweet spot. By now I'm sure you've come across one or two TED Talk videos online, but what many people don't know is that the very first TED Talk in 1984 was a combination of technology, entertainment, and design and included a demo of the compact disc (CD), the e-book, and 3-D graphics. As you can imagine, the event didn't do so well, and they actually lost money. It wasn't until 1990 that the founders would try the conference out again, but this time they would bring a new roster of presenters who represented a broad range of industries, appealing to an audience who shared the traits of curiosity and open-mindedness. In 2001, TED was bought out and turned into a nonprofit, with new changes that included starting an audio and video podcast series, TED Talks, where the best TED content would be released free online. In just over two months, those six podcasts reached more than one million views. By providing its audience with free access to some of the world's greatest thinkers, leaders, and teachers, TED became a household name, and according to the TED website, by 2012, TED Talks celebrated its one billionth video view.

CREATING MEANINGFUL CONTENT

To build relationships with people in an already crowded space, you will need to present content that has both meaning and purpose. Lyfe Marketing issued a report highlighting that 78 percent of consumers prefer getting to know a company via articles rather than ads, and 70 percent believe that organizations providing custom content are interested in building good relationships with them.[1] Good content can build trust and establish credibility. By explaining your company's points of differentiation, you are allowing the product or service to sell itself. You are showing how you are innovative without actually saying you are an "innovator." It's similar to when a company claims to be the "best"; naturally, no one will believe them. You have to allow consumers to develop their own perception of you. By providing consumers with quality content that is insightful and factual, you are meeting them halfway. You are presenting information that is waiting to be perceived.

One great thing about content is that it is cost-effective. There are minimal fees involved with getting your choice of platform up and running. Figuring out how to do this is easy. Thanks to the Internet, there are an endless number of how-to videos you can reference. In terms of content development, there are websites like UpWork, Fiverr, and Guru that have thousands of specialists available for one-time projects. Vetting the individual for your specific project may take some time, but with candidate profiles, reviews, and success rates included on each specialist, you'll have a good idea of who the person is before you hire them. Once you work with them on one or two projects, you will be able to judge if you like their work or not, and they will get to know you and what you expect, so it becomes an easier process to work with them more regularly.

COMMUNICATION CHANNELS: THE DIFFERENT FORMS OF MESSAGE DELIVERY

The Internet has provided us with an endless number of forums that allow us to reach a larger audience with our thoughts and creative content. The forum that will work best for your company will be based on your company goals. If you specialize in legal services, for example, your audience likely consists of thought leaders who are consistently searching for new reading content. These individuals are more left-brain dominant and more analytical and methodical in their thinking. Platforms like a blog or Twitter will be better received by them, as it will stimulate deep thoughts and conversations, rather than Instagram or video, which is targeted more toward the right-brain dominant person who is more creative and visual based.

Blogs

A platform for establishing yourself as an expert voice, blogs provide you with the opportunity to express your thoughts, opinions, and suggestions all in one place. According to HubSpot, blogs are among the three primary forms of media used in content strategies today.

A blog can live directly on your website or as a standalone site. A blog on your website will help increase your visibility online, or what is often referred to as your *search engine optimization* (SEO). The better visibility you have, the more likely you will appear higher up in search results. A blog on your company website should have its own tab within the toolbar labeled "blog," or you can give it its own name, like startup Republic, an open investment platform, did with their blog called *Journal*, which is subdivided into topics relevant to their brand.

While developing content for your blog, you'll want to be conscious of length and utilization of select keywords. Your audience inputs these select words or phrases into search engines like Google to find websites related to your company. How quickly you come up in the search engine will be related to how often you use those keywords on your website. There are numerous websites that can help you research the best keywords, including Soovle, Jaax, and Ahrefs Keywords Explorer. To see how your website effectively ranks, Google Search Console provides you with a performance report on how well you rank with each specific keyword. In terms of article length, SEMrush reports that articles that are fewer than three thousand words get three times more traffic, four times the number of shares, and three and a half times more backlinks than other articles.[2]

Video

While video may seem intimidating because it involves more production time, Statista reports that each month 85 percent of Internet users in the US watch video content.[3] If a video lives on the homepage of your website, you'll want it to look more polished and professionally produced, which requires the hiring of an outside specialist. For content that lives on platforms other than your homepage, you can use your smartphone or a webcam to produce it with an off-the-cuff feel that comes across as authentic and relatable. If you're looking for software to help you edit these videos, check out Premiere Pro, Final Cut Pro X, and Premiere Elements.

As we talked about earlier, the mindless scrolling caused by social media has reduced attention spans, causing industry professionals to adapt their content to be shorter. For videos, it's best to keep them on the shorter side and focus on capturing the viewer's engagement within the first thirty seconds. Typically, videos that are longer involve a question-and-answer (Q&A) format where the host invites an outside guest to be on the program and they are interviewed with a series of questions. Videos can live on a YouTube channel, which you can embed the links to on your own webpage. Other video formats include a video blog (vlog), webinars, and live streaming on a social media channel. Internet personality Gary Vaynerchuk—also

an entrepreneur, *New York Times* best-selling author, and speaker—
is known for his engaging video content that is distributed almost
daily on his YouTube channel. His vlogs provide viewers with raw
insight into a day in the life of an entrepreneur while providing
advice to others in their journey. His YouTube channel alone has
nearly three million subscribers, in addition to his Instagram and
Twitter pages, where he also pushes out the content.

Whatever content you produce, start out by determining your
goals. For example, do you want to educate people about a topic?
Or do you want to entertain them? Will it be a regular series, and
should there be a pithy name for it? Will there be a set host, and
will they be talking about a specific topic each time, or will they
interview regular guests? You'll also want to find a way to engage
the viewer, whether it be by requesting they participate in a live
discussion, comment, or ask questions. One thing to avoid when
developing your content is coming across like a salesperson. Instead,
focus on providing value with insightful information and let your
company's expertise sell itself. Whatever content you create, you'll
want to ensure that the look, feel, and tone are consistent with the
branding of your business and that you are sharing the content on
all your social media channels.

Podcasts

According to a report by Edison Research, roughly ninety million
people listen to a podcast each month. You don't have to be tech savvy
to create a podcast.[4] You don't even need a sound studio. Technology
today allows you to create great-sounding audio straight from the

comfort of your own home or office. There are also how-to guides online to help you through the process from start to finish. They'll help you choose the best audio equipment, get you set up with an intro/outro, and even tell you where to upload all the files to.

When you decide to launch a podcast, the theme you pick should tie back to your business and its core values. You don't want it to feel too promotional, so it's better not to have the podcast be entirely about your company. Instead, find a unique way to talk about the industry. Search through the podcasts available on iTunes and Spotify for your genre. Is there something not being discussed that you could fill that void with? And is it something that you can develop one hundred-plus topics with? You can always generate more content when there are more people involved. Will you have a cohost? Are you interviewing guests? Or perhaps you and your colleagues are sitting around discussing a topic at great length?

LinkedIn

An excellent tool for professional networking, LinkedIn, according to a HubSpot report, has nearly seven hundred million users at the time of this writing.[5] As LinkedIn continues to evolve its features, it has become much more than just a place to connect with like-minded individuals. LinkedIn has become a popular social media platform for brands to present themselves as a company, what they do, and why it's important enough to follow their updates. It's similar to what a website does, but on a platform that supports interaction and engagement. A company that uses LinkedIn to its fullest extent is Greenhouse Software, the fastest-growing provider of enterprise talent acquisition software. Because their profile is colorful, with an eye-catching photo as their banner, an edgy tagline, and content that is posted regularly with a colorful visual component, they are able to grab the attention of their reader and stand out from the standard text profiles that exist on LinkedIn. Images generally see two times as many comments, while video is five times more likely to spark a conversation than any other type of content shared on LinkedIn.[6]

With LinkedIn, not only can you share third-party links; you can also create and share your own original articles. Here you can discuss innovation and touch on the pain points of what you do while also adding in the human factor, making it a great platform to establish thought leadership for not only your brand but also you as the founder. The *2020 B2B Thought Leadership Impact Study*, issued by LinkedIn, confirms that brands that succeed in building a culture of thought leadership have better reputations and higher sales figures.[7]

Your personal LinkedIn page is connected to your business, since the business is listed as your current position. Before you get started sharing content on your own page, make sure the page is optimized with current information. An up-to-date headshot and a banner image relative to your business are the first things someone will notice when they click through to your page. Next is a tagline that is both insightful and engaging. As someone scrolls through, they'll notice the "About" section, which should be one to two paragraphs in length.

Your work experience should be up to date, with a paragraph description of the work you did at each company. The longest description will be for your current position at your startup company. Here you can also add links or upload media, so you can include recent press you've been featured in, any articles they've written, or any external documents, photos, sites, videos, and presentations. Then you'll want to include your education, volunteer work, and interests, which is the most personal you'll get on LinkedIn. In the "Skills & endorsements" section, list any words that best represent your capabilities.

Once you start writing articles or secure media placements during your PR outreach, you'll want to list them in the "Featured" section. This section will provide you with an added level of credibility, as it stands out among the rest when you scroll. Liz Ryan, founder and CEO of Human Workplace, a publishing and consulting firm, regularly posts new content and receives over 178,000 views and 6,800-plus comments. Her articles relate to her work in human resources, so her blogs include topics like "When Is It Too Late to Change Careers?" and "Do You Have to Break Rules to Get a Good Job?"

Twitter

With LinkedIn, one post a day is sufficient, but with Twitter you can post as much as you like. The 280 characters allow you to share concise thoughts, ask a question, talk to someone directly by tagging them, or even promote your company. Twitter encourages engagement, so it allows customers to ask questions instantaneously without having to pick up a phone and call a customer service line. You'll also be able to gain greater awareness of your customer insights by seeing how people are talking about you. In terms of branding on Twitter, make sure your icon photo and banner are properly sized and are within your brand's color scheme. You can also use the same photos across all social media channels to ensure there is cohesive brand recognition. The username you select can also be the same across all channels, if applicable. If the username you want isn't available, try something similar—like Republic, who uses @joinrepublic.

You can also use Twitter for your founder's thought leadership, as it provides you a platform to offer a unique perspective while people listen and ask insightful questions of you as an expert in your field. You can also follow other thought leaders and engage with them in one-on-one conversations that anyone following either of you can see. Tagging someone in your Tweet is beneficial because it opens up the opportunity for the other person to "Retweet" you, meaning they will repost your Tweet to their Twitter page. Twitter's Retweet feature helps you and others quickly share that Tweet with all your followers. You can Retweet your own Tweets or Tweets from someone else.

You can plan some of your content in advance, which allows you to have it readily available to be shared. The Retweets and the replies can happen in real time, but you can use platforms like Hootsuite to schedule and share curated content without having to go on Twitter every day to do so. The curated content can be personal quotes, blogs you've created for your website, links to your latest podcast, articles from LinkedIn, or even links to articles from third parties, such as a media outlet. Content that you can share in real time includes thoughts relative to breaking news, replies to other thought leaders' Tweets, and quotes from speakers at conferences or events. When sharing your personal thoughts, you'll want to be mindful that whatever you put out will be a representation of your brand. This is not a place to post about political opinions that will engage one side and alienate the other. Save that banter for your personal circle of friends and family.

Because Twitter limits you to a select number of characters in each Tweet, when you share a link, you'll want to first run it through the website Bitly, a shortening service and link-management platform. You'll also want to include hashtags at the end of your Tweet. Be realistic with what you hashtag; it should be words that are commonly used and that already have results when searched. It is recommended that you use two hashtags in each Tweet. And be sure to avoid any spaces or punctuation in a hashtag, or it will not work properly.

Facebook

According to Pew Research Center, roughly two-thirds of US adults report that they are Facebook users, which explains why Facebook is the primary content-distribution channel for marketers today.[8] It's a platform that you can count on a large portion of your audience being connected to. It's almost become a requirement for all businesses to have a Facebook page. And if you don't have one, you can sure bet your competition does. Facebook fosters communities, so for a business, it's a great place to gather your customers, your fans, and any prospects to provide reviews, post questions, share opinions, join in on a conversation, and offer personal feedback.

One mistake I see businesses often make is using a personal profile as their business page versus creating an actual Facebook business page. Aside from the difference in look and feel between the two, it also violates Facebook's policies on using a personal profile for commercial or promotional purposes, and you run the risk of your account being deleted. The easiest way to tell if your page is a personal one is if it asks people to add you as a "friend"; with a business page, people can "like" your page. As you set up your Facebook business page, make sure to select a page template that suits your industry. There are specific templates for restaurants, venues, services, shopping, general business, and so on.

Facebook can provide you a window into your customer insights by offering Page Insights to help you understand the actions people are taking on your page. You can learn what they care about and how often they interact with specific posts on your page, which will help you understand the type of content they like. Facebook, similar to Twitter and Instagram, allows you to create a username, which, again, should be the same as the others or very similar. For JMGPR, we use @JMGPublicRelations, which can also be written out as www.facebook.com/jmgpublicrelations. Once you have your profile updated with key information and graphics and you have a few posts already up, you can start to explore Facebook ads, which can be targeted to customers within as close as a ten- to fifteen-mile radius.

Instagram

The most visual of all the social media channels, Instagram is a photo-sharing platform that has high engagement among its followers. For companies, that means you can quickly develop a loyal brand following. To get started, you will want to make sure that your profile is set to a business account, not a personal, and all account information is added and up to date. Because people are coming to Instagram to look at photos, you'll want to make sure all visuals shared are high quality and tell a cohesive story. You can tell if it's cohesive when you look at the grid after a photo is uploaded. The *grid* refers to the layout of all your photos shown together on your profile. The colors of all the photos should blend with each other and have common themes among the content you post. For JMGPR, we focus on New York City–related content, the quintessential PR Girl with behind-the-scenes content, and pops of pink and white throughout. For your brand, you'll want to create a visual aesthetic that best relates to your identity and core values.

When you post your photo with a clear and concise description, be sure to add in hashtags at the end of your caption. To encourage higher engagement, select hashtags that other people will search. For instance, if you are a restaurant, you'll want to use hashtags like #food, #foodie, #yummy, #bar, #dinner, #foodporn. If you looked up each of these hashtags individually, you'd see that they have millions of photos from other people who used that same tag. As you search through the hashtags and click through to people's profiles, you can start to become familiar with who may be a potential customer for you. When you find those people, it's best to engage by liking and commenting on their photos and even following them if you want to see more. Those people will also be doing the same. So if you use hashtags that are more search-friendly, it is more likely they will come across you.

Instagram is continuously adding more business-friendly features, like IGTV, which provides long-form vertical video on Instagram.

This allows users to share live video content between fifteen and sixteen minutes long. Instagram Reels is another fun way to create videos to share on Instagram. You can record and edit fifteen-second multi-clip videos with audio, effects, and new creative tools.

Newsletter

A newsletter is another cost-effective method for sharing new content you created. It provides your business with the opportunity to increase awareness, promote your products or services, and demonstrate your expertise in the field. A newsletter can also generate leads and sales that will help your business to scale. If your website domain is hosted on Squarespace, they have a feature built into the platform that allows you to develop and distribute newsletters. There are also standalone sites focused entirely on the newsletter-making process, like MailChimp or Emma.

When developing content, HubSpot suggests balancing your newsletter content to be 90 percent educational and 10 percent promotional. Pick one theme for the newsletter so all content included is cohesive and representative of the one major message you want to convey. Keep your newsletters concise with summaries of the new content you developed and links to "learn more" on another platform (e.g., the blog on your website). You can measure the success of your newsletter by considering how many people opened your email, how many clicked on links within it, and how many people unsubscribed to it. (Hey, it happens. Try not to take it personally.)

Table 3.1 is a quick point of reference to best summarize all the communication channels discussed here.

Table 3.1: Summary of communication channels

Channel	Hashtags	Photos: 300 dpi	Suggested frequency	Type of audience
Blogs	✓	✓	Biweekly or monthly	Thought leader
Video		✓	Biweekly or monthly	Creative
Podcast			Biweekly or monthly	Thought leader
LinkedIn		✓	Daily	Thought leader
Twitter	✓	✓	Daily	Thought leader
Facebook		✓	Daily	Thought leader/ creative
Instagram	✓	✓	Daily	Thought leader/ creative
Newsletter		✓	Biweekly or monthly	Thought leader/ creative

STAY ON POINT: CREATING CONTENT THAT ALIGNS WITH YOUR BRAND IDENTITY

The most important thing to keep in mind when issuing content is that the content needs to align with your brand identity. We previously worked with a real estate company to do an overhaul on their social media profiles, and prior to working with us they posted on their Instagram page a photo that described how to properly pick up after your dog. You could make the argument that too many people let their dogs use other people's grass to poop, so it's somewhat real estate specific, but it's not the job of the real estate company to tell you that. Their focus is on selling you beautiful homes in a specific regional market. Once we started to work together, we deleted the dog poop photo, among many others, and now the page is filled with interior and exterior images of homes, as well as photos of the surrounding neighborhood, so that the agency can now be the authority on life in that market.

As you develop content for each of your platforms, consider who the audience is on each platform; what your competitors are doing, so you can do it differently; and how you can provide value without coming across as a salesperson. One way to avoid the latter is by being authentic from the start. Your core values should always be ingrained in everything you do, so ask yourself if the content you are about to issue is aligned with your brand's beliefs. Does it take into consideration the *human effect*? Are you creating a personable experience for the reader that adds value to their everyday life? You will also want to consider how you are conveying your innovation to your reader so that they understand why you are the leader of your category. Last, are you addressing the "why" factor, targeting the pain points of your reader, and offering a solution for them?

FOLLOW THE CARDINAL RULE: DON'T SPAM

We learned earlier that *noise* refers to the excessive amount of information available in the world, but noise isn't just about the overwhelming amount of information put out by others. You can also make too much of your own noise, which can lead customers to feel overwhelmed. One thing to keep in mind when issuing new content is that you don't want to spam people. Fun fact: The name *spam*, also known as junk mail, came from a Monty Python sketch in which the food Spam is ubiquitous, unavoidable, and repetitive. You don't want customers feeling like your content—just like Spam—is ubiquitous, unavoidable, and repetitive. Instead, spread out the content with a strategic plan developed in advance. You can break your content calendar down by month and then by week. For instance, how many articles do you want to write a month? To ease into the process, you can start with one, and for social media, you can start with posting two to three times a week.

PLAN AHEAD: CREATING YOUR CONTENT CALENDAR

As you build out content for your channels, you will want to figure out a schedule to keep it organized and manageable. It will also prevent you from missing post dates and from posting content that wasn't strategically thought out or intentional. Websites like Monday.com and HubSpot have template calendars available, but you can also create your own based on what days of the week you'll want to post and how often. You can even overlap some of your content for a few of your social media channels. One thing to keep in mind: Make sure to stop scheduled content during national emergencies or national breaking news. Social media allows for instant feedback, so if you post something about "saving the world" with your product, for example, and it's the beginning of the pandemic, your message most likely will not be well received.

LONGEVITY: GETTING THE MOST OUT OF YOUR CONTENT

The goal after creating new material is to get as much mileage as you can out of it and to maximize the type of exposure you can get from it. After a particular piece of content is rolled out, it's important to continue riding the wave and generate as much buzz as possible within your respective community. If you're wondering why creating additional attention is necessary, the simple answer is you want to show others that people are talking about you and your business. By extending the life of the original placement in a variety of ways, you'll gain even more of an ROI. While it sounds pretty simple and straightforward, surprisingly many people do not take that extra step to share new content across as many platforms as possible. By not doing more, you're in fact missing out on the traffic and conversations that the information could generate.

The objective is to take whatever content you created on one platform and not only share it but also craft something new from it. What you want to do is generate more views, maximize exposure, and attract an audience of your own. Social media is an excellent tool to help spread the word to a wider audience. If you're concerned people will get bored seeing the same information across numerous outlets, don't be. Instead of just hitting Share, you can customize the post for each social media platform by tweaking the description, swapping images, or using different hashtags. Think about creating your own caption or lead-in to briefly explain exactly what it is people are about to see (or read). Perhaps there's a particular quote within the piece you can highlight directly in the caption. The goal is to grab attention so whoever is scrolling past will want to see what you're sharing.

Consider highlighting your content directly on your website. To make it visually aesthetic, choose a graphic you can click on that links to the story or video. You can also add social media share buttons that will make the process simple for visitors to reshare content; the easier you make it, the more likely they'll do it. If there are clients, vendors, customers, or anyone connected to your business who would be interested in your thoughts and content, send an email or newsletter with a direct link to the placement. For our clients at JMGPR, whatever content we create for them, we continuously stress the importance of using that information as a building block to further establish the company as a leader in the industry.

❮❮ Innovation Station ❯❯

Now that you've received the full lowdown on content development, it's time to start planning! To get started, make sure you have the profiles claimed for your company on all social media channels and that you have all the categories of the profile updated accordingly. Next, you'll want to determine which channels you'll want to focus more energy on. Think about your customer and where they look for new information. Are they scrolling through Instagram and veering toward the more creative and visually designed elements of content? Or are they readers that enjoy a long-form article with lots of nuggets of information?

Next, how are you being innovative in the content you are providing? What are your competitors doing, and how can you offer a fresh approach? Content development is tied to your brand identity. It's in the short moments when someone sees your content that you have to offer a good first impression, so use each word carefully and each color strategically to make a strong statement.

{ Part II }

BUILD

CHAPTER 4

Brand Materials

Communication works for those who work at it.

—ATTRIBUTED TO JOHN POWELL

The materials you use to promote your business are called your brand's *assets*. These assets are extremely valuable to your brand. Without these materials, you will struggle to gain brand recognition. And without brand recognition, it will be much harder to sell your products and services, because yours will seem like everyone else's.

We've had numerous companies sign on for PR who were in a rush to get quick media hits, and understandably so. We're all excited to start seeing our name in the press. But what these companies didn't realize, until it was explained, is that the press materials are crucial to their success in achieving media placements. You simply can't rush good materials. If you do, you run the risk of sending mixed messaging and appearing disorganized. There's nothing worse than receiving a request for press materials and having to scramble to get them together at the last second.

When someone asks you to email them more information about your company, you don't want to just send them a link to your website. That is impersonal and forces them to look for the information they want about you. Instead, give them a packet of key information about your company that summarizes some of the content on your website. These assets that you create for prospective clients or customers are the modern-day "brochure." The information in these packets, however, is more strategic and less salesy.

For instance, if a reporter asks for one of your founder's bios, they are referring to a one-page document, also known as a *one-sheet*, that will give them top-line information about the person's background. For startup companies, these assets don't have to be just for media relations purposes; they can also be materials you share with potential investors, potential customers, and even your internal team. People can also be considered an asset to your company, as they can be spokespeople and speak on behalf of the brand. How you develop and present these assets is part of the public relations process covered in this book.

THE PRESS KIT

Public relations is like a beautiful package. It pulls together key items that you want to gift to someone and covers them in wrapping that is visually appealing and provides a good first impression. In PR, that package is called your *press kit*. When we work with new clients, we go through what we call "ramp-up," in which we develop all the materials we need in our arsenal to make for a successful relationship. Traditionally, a press kit was a printout of top-line information relevant to your brand that was handed to editors and producers for consideration. Now, thanks to the Internet, we use electronic press kits, better known as EPKs, which include embedded links to video examples and websites. We generally build out the EPK during the first one to three weeks of working together. That way, no one is scrambling to compile materials when a request comes in for them.

One-Line Description

Your company needs a strong one-sentence description that sums up who you are and what you offer without going into the full thirty-second "elevator pitch." According to their Facebook page, Uber "helps millions of people move toward opportunity every day in over 700 cities around the world," while Robinhood is "democratizing finance for all," and DoorDash "empowers small business owners to offer delivery in an affordable and convenient way." At JMGPR, we are serving innovators and their mission-driven startup companies. To create your one-liner, use the following format developed by the Founder Institute.[1]

> [Startup name] is developing [a defined offering] to help [a target audience] [solve a problem] [with your "secret sauce"].

About Page

As experts living in the day-to-day grind, you can probably spend hours talking about what you do, so much so that condensing it down into one page can be an extremely hard task. The "About" page—better known as the *one-pager*, or, in marketing, a *sell sheet*—is a description of your company, highlighting the most important information that people need to know. Its job is to start the conversation so that if someone wants more information about a given item listed, they will ask you for it. Think of it as your thirty-second pitch in written form with a few supporting facts to back it up.

You can't possibly say everything you want to say in the one-pager, so don't try to. The goal with a one-pager is to provide an overview of your company while capturing the attention of your reader. The information you provide must be strategic, including items like key differentiators or innovations that will automatically distinguish you from competitors. You also don't want to be too text heavy to the point where you don't leave any white space. You don't want the reader to feel overwhelmed or think it will take too long for them to read through; rather, you want them to think it's a quick read and worth the glance over.

After the content, the next most important part of the one-pager is the layout. If you use images, don't make them so big that they overpower the page; it might look as if you're trying to compensate for a lack of talking points. The page also needs to be easy to read and attractive enough to read. This is where you can contract a designer to create a look that will help you to stand out. Websites like UpWork and Fiverr are a great source for this. The color scheme and fonts should be the same as what your company typically uses in their branding and should mirror your online collateral, such as your website, blog, and social media pages.

Include the following in your one-pager:

- Your logo with the company name

- The one-liner you developed previously

- A paragraph that addresses the who, what, when, where, why, and how

  - Start with the year the company was developed.

  - Who started the company?

  - Why was it started (what problem were you trying to solve)?

  - What do you do differently (specifically addressing how you are different from your competitors)?

- Three to five of the top specifications (specs) about your product or service, including any relevant data points. If there's a product, include an image of the product.

- Any research you have available to show how your company is a necessity right now

- Any recent awards and accolades

Product Sheet

While the About page mentions the products and highlights the most important or impressive highlights, the *product sheet* will include more of the specific details. For the companies that are selling one to five products, a product sheet will provide readers with a snapshot of their key descriptors. If you have more than five products, it may seem more like a catalogue, so try to select five or so options as "products to spotlight," rather than trying to cram everything into your product sheet.

On the product sheet, you'll also want to include images of each of the products being discussed, their prices, and their name and key features. At the end, create a call to action and include where and how the products can be purchased and who to contact for more information. Remember, the product sheet for the press kit isn't going to your target audience. This is specifically meant for media people and can potentially be used for other purposes, such as sending to investors or high-level individuals who want to learn more about your company. Based on this, you don't want to put generic contact information on your materials. If you are the sole employee, then list your information. If you have someone you can rely on that you know will answer calls or emails, then use them. Include their name, title, phone number, and email address.

Fact Sheet

If your company has been in business for several years, you likely have numerous milestones that may need to be mapped out and clearly explained for readers on—you guessed it—a *one-sheet*, also known as *fact sheet*. Here you can build a timeline, starting from when the company was launched, and include key dates leading up to today. Some items to include are awards and recognitions, key products or feature launches, acquisitions, and funding. You don't need to go into great detail about each; just the mention of it works, or you can include a few key words if needed.

Bios

Not everyone who works for your company needs a bio in the press kit. This section is for the individuals who will act as spokespeople on behalf of the brand. They are people who are comfortable speaking with the media, are fully versed in your company's history, and can answer any product- or service-related questions. Often this is the founder of the company or someone in the C-suite. Whoever it is, you always want these individuals to have excellent communication skills. They should have the ability to remain calm under pressure and the know-how to navigate difficult questions, so much so that the person listening can confidently trust the representative and, therefore, your company.

If you are an early-stage startup, there likely won't be any surprise or negative questions or anything that would spark a controversy, so your spokesperson doesn't need to be highly media trained just yet. The experience will come with practice. If you are a mid-stage startup or later, then you will want your spokespeople to have more experience in media relations.

Your bio is meant to be a personal narrative explaining all the steps that led up to where you are today, at your company. It is not a résumé, full of facts and information in short sentences. Instead, the bio is meant to be a story that emphasizes the value you bring in your work. Often I'll read a client's bio and find adjectives like *exceptional, successful,* and *groundbreaking.* You want to avoid using superlative adjectives (an example of this would be "the *best* interior designer in Manhattan"), because it comes across as if you are trying to compensate for something. If you lead with the facts, the words speak for themselves. At the end of the bio, you can also add a few personal details about yourself, which shows there's more to you than just the business side. When creating your bio, include the following:

- Name and title

- If you are the founder, then the year you started the company. If you aren't, then the year you joined.

- One line about the company and what it does

- The company/companies that you worked for previously
  - What was your job function there?
  - Major accomplishments while there? Did you increase revenue by X percent or launch an international campaign doing XYZ?

- Any certifications?

- Volunteer work? Do you serve on any boards?

- Where did you attend college/grad school/any other advanced studies? And what are your degrees in?

- The last one to two sentences of the bio should be a personal snapshot of you, highlighting something that makes you unique.
  - What city/state do you reside in?
  - What do you like to do on the weekends (biking, hiking, cooking, etc.)?
  - Do you have kids?

Boilerplate

A *boilerplate* is a short summary about your company that consists of approximately three to four sentences. It is often inserted at the end of a press release as a quick summary of the company's top-level information. A media person may even ask for a short blurb about the company before they consider reviewing the full materials that are typically lengthier.

The boilerplate is often used when the one-liner is too short and the one-pager is too long. It can best be compared to the thirty-second elevator pitch, just with websites and social media handles included. Here's the one Orangetheory uses:

> Orangetheory® (www.orangetheory.com) makes it simple to get More Life from your workout. One of the world's fastest-growing franchise companies, Orangetheory has developed a unique approach to fitness that blends a unique trifecta of science, coaching and technology that work together seamlessly to elevate participants' heart rates to help burn more calories. Backed by the science of excess post-exercise oxygen consumption (EPOC), Orangetheory workouts incorporate endurance, strength and power to generate the "Orange Effect," whereby participants keep burning calories for up to 24 hours after a 60-minute workout. Orangetheory franchisees have opened over 1,400 studios in all 50 U.S. states and 25 countries. The company was ranked #60 in Inc. magazine's Fastest

Growing Private Companies list and was listed as #9 on the 2020 Entrepreneur Fastest-Growing Franchise 500 list. Visit www.otffranchise.com for global franchise opportunities.[2]

To make this even better, I would add hyperlinks to the company's website and links to their social media channels at the end. This helps the reader, as they don't have to do the work themselves by clicking and searching for the company's social media channels.

Use the following template to create your boilerplate:

- *Sentence 1:* Include your mission. What does your business do exactly?

- *Sentence 2:* What is your market differentiator? How is your company different from anyone else out there? What is the key benefit that you offer?

- *Sentence 3:* Any facts to support your claim above?

- *Sentence 4:* Provide company statistics.

  - Did you receive funding (e.g., you recently raised your $12 million in your Series A for a total of $32 million in funding to date)?

  - Do you have a large and impressive number of customers (e.g., your app that has over five million users in ten countries)?

- *Sentence 5:* Any outstanding awards and recognitions? If so, mention the names of the awards all in one sentence.

- *Sentence 6:* Link to your website and any social media channels. Here's what ours looks like:

> For additional information, please visit www. jmgpublicrelations.com or visit us on Instagram @jmg_pr and on Facebook @jmgpublicrelations.

If you don't have responses to sentences 3 and 4, then your boilerplate will be condensed down to four sentences. The boilerplate should be one paragraph and not multiple ones with spaces in between. Also, don't exaggerate or include information that you don't have facts to back up.

Digital Artwork

Photos are important to today's visually focused world. People scroll through social media and look at photos all day long. The artwork you create should always look professional. That doesn't mean you have to hire a photographer for every single photo you take, but for the core images that represent your brand and that can be used continuously as a visual narrative, you will want professional help. All images should be 300 dpi (dots per inch). Anything lower than that and the photo can look pixelated or blurry, which can come across as low quality. Today's cell phones are a great option for photos that will only be used once in a blog post or as Instagram content, but for headshots or product photos that will be used more than once, you will want to invest in someone who can produce high-quality images for you.

The images that you will need in your press kit include the following:

- Company logos

- Headshots of each spokesperson, with a bio

- If you offer a product, you'll want to include product shots. If you have over ten products, then select the top five to ten to highlight.

- If you have an app, include screengrabs of the app in use. Also include images of an actual phone with the app open.

- If you are on a SaaS platform, include screengrabs of the platform itself.

The photos could all be displayed in the actual EPK, or you could also provide a link to a digital library for downloading. This way, with one quick click, an editor or producer can easily download the assets to their computer. The easier you can make the process for them, the more likely it is they will continue to work with you.

Press Features

Including media placements (a term that can be interchanged with *press placements*) within the press kit allows you to show off what other people are saying about you. This gives you an added level of credibility, because if a media person took the time to recognize your brand enough to write a full story about you, then to others seeing this, you are worth reviewing for their own considerations, too. For this section, it's always better to include more than less. Media placements hold a lot of weight, so having more than one media placement to show will only add to your credibility. Within the press kit, each media hit should have its own page. This is often referred to as a *press clipping*. At the top of each page, include the logo of the media outlet. Below that should be a screenshot of the title of the article and then how the feature looks; if the entire story is about you, then the entire story should be featured.

If you are mentioned in only a portion of a very long article, then include only a screenshot of that paragraph, and the same for images. Once you start to accumulate an abundance of press placements, then you can sift through and categorize them by the quality of media outlet and the quality of the media placement. If you were mentioned in a lesser-known publication, then perhaps don't include that press clipping. Instead, opt for a media outlet that's more recognizable. The more well-known a media outlet, the harder it is to be featured in it. It's more competitive and thus more impressive to someone scrolling through your EPK.

Final Materials

Once the materials are developed, you can save each document as an individual file in case you need just one of the items, and you can also package them together nicely into a PDF. This PDF will be the completed EPK. It should have a cover page that includes a company photo and contact information should someone want to coordinate an interview or simply learn more about the company.

THE WEBSITE

Have you ever gone to a website and even after reading the few lines on the homepage, you still can't figure out what that company does? It's usually because they try to make what they do sound fancier than it is, or they use such complex words that the average reader can't understand the brand's true identity. Did you stay on the page? Or did you move on? Chances are, unless you were preparing for a job interview or needed something specific from the page, you moved on. And if you were a media outlet that could have promoted that business, they would have just lost some good press.

To avoid this situation for your own business, you should capture a website visitor's attention within the first few seconds. If the viewer is bored or confused right away, they certainly won't click around trying to figure things out and will likely exit your website. Ensure the words and images you present on your homepage clearly depict your brand. The messaging on your site should present a problem, create a solution, and be creative enough in its word usage to show that you are presenting something much bigger to the world and that you aren't just selling a product. The press materials you generated earlier will help ensure your messaging is being told cohesively, so it won't matter if someone reads it on your one-pager or on your website.

Your website is an important piece of your public relations strategy because, in addition to the EPK, a media person will do their due diligence and visit your company website. If there's inconsistent messaging between the EPK and the website, they will either ask you to clarify or move on to another company so they don't have to do so much back-and-forth to obtain the information they need.

Another reason your website is important is because it is another channel for perception. The people going to your website are likely clients/customers, investors, and potential media people. You want them to understand instantly who your brand is without having to click around your website to figure it out. To accomplish this, make your message clear, understandable, and most importantly, up front.

Within the "Contact" section of your website, it's always a good idea to list out the point of contact for a reporter. This enables them to reach someone should they want to do an interview. A general email works for the "For Press Inquiries" section. Just confirm someone is on the receiving end of these email notifications so there isn't a delay in response or, worse, a lost email, and you potentially miss an opportunity for a big press feature.

You can also build out a section of your website for press assets. That way, if a writer wants to go to your website to find more information for a story they are on a deadline for, they won't have to contact you for it. You can create a tab at the top or very bottom of the page for press inquiries. On the "Press Inquiries" page, you can list out each of the assets you created and include a hyperlink for download. You can even create a larger library that can include an endless number of photos. When doing so, be sure to keep them neatly organized by name and category.

👣 Innovation Station 👣

With the changes that happen so quickly in a startup, the trends that come in and out, and the fast-changing news cycles, information can become outdated fast. It's important to update and reassess press materials and key messaging every six months. This information will also help develop your voice for the content you create for your social media channels, which should also be reassessed regularly. While building your press materials, it's very easy to get into "salesperson mode" with the overuse of buzzwords and superlatives, but unless you want to sound as if you are compensating for something and trying to appear bigger than you are, don't give in to that impulse. Remember, less is more. Chances are, if you are starting a new company, you are offering something unique to the market that you feel hasn't been done before. If that's the case, then you represent innovation at its finest, so make sure the words used to describe you demonstrate that.

CHAPTER 5

Great Storytelling

The most powerful person in the world is the storyteller.

—STEVE JOBS, CEO of Pixar, to his team in the break room, 1994

A cowboy—yes, a cowboy (bear with me here)—rode into town and stopped at a saloon for a drink. Unfortunately, the locals always had a habit of picking on strangers, which he was. When he finished his drink, he found that his horse had been stolen. He went back into the bar, handily flipped his gun into the air, caught it above his head without even looking, and fired a shot into the ceiling. "Which one of you sidewinders stole my horse?!" he yelled with surprising forcefulness. No one answered. "All right, I'm gonna have another beer, and if my horse ain't back outside by the time I finish, I'm gonna do what I done in Texas! And I don't like to have to do what I done in Texas!" Some of the locals shifted restlessly. The man, true to his word, had another beer and walked outside, and his horse had been returned to the post. He saddled up and started to ride out of town. The bartender wandered out of the bar and asked, "Say, partner, before you go, . . . what happened in Texas?" The cowboy turned back and said, "I had to walk home."

Storytelling is the ability to paint a picture through your words. In the old joke shared here, the strange cowboy walks into a bar filled with locals, and while he is having a drink, his horse is stolen. Because all these different elements were introduced within the first three sentences of the story, you were instantly hooked and wanted to find out why the strange cowboy was there, what the locals would do, and what the heck happened to that horse! The story is engaging and creates a sense of mystery.

Storytelling is about catching the attention of and then captivating your listener. The five elements of a traditional story consist of the characters, the setting, the plot, conflict, and a resolution. In business, though, there aren't always stories that involve cowboys and horses or that are overly exciting or super sexy. You also can't use too much of your imagination, because you don't want your customer to feel as though you are overcompensating or overselling your product or service.

For business purposes, your story should include the following:

- *Plot:* How did you discover your innovation?

- *Conflict:* Did you come across a problem in your day-to-day personal life that you realized needed solving? And was there nothing on the market that could solve it for you?

- *Setting:* What were the circumstances surrounding your discovery? Did a family member's illness spark your idea, or was there something happening in world news that spoke to you?

- *Resolution:* What did you create as the solution? Who else was involved?

- *Customers:* Who is the target market for this? Is there a statistic you can include here to show the level of impact your product will have? For instance, does that problem affect five million Americans?

ELEVATOR PITCH

Networking is the bane of many entrepreneurs' existence. On top of your day-to-day work, you spend numerous hours each week connecting with and meeting new people. You hope for that one perfect conversation that leads into a direct sale (yes, love when that happens!) or an intro to someone who can potentially be your customer. Regardless of whether you like it or not, networking is key to growing your business. Seventy-seven percent of consumers are more likely to buy a new product if they learn about it from friends or family (Word of Mouth Marketing Association), which is why it's important to make a good first impression.[1] There's a reason it's called the "elevator pitch." The name derives from the short amount of time you have between floors when riding an elevator with someone. After you deliver your short pitch, the person decides if they walk out of the elevator and never see you again, or if they hold the door so they can ask for your business card to continue the conversation at a later time.

Your elevator pitch should be customer focused and last around thirty seconds. It should include the plot, conflict, setting, and resolution. One of the biggest challenges the innovators we work with face is that they are so excited about their work that they can't condense their story down to a few simple sound bites. In their minds, *all* the information is pertinent to understanding their full story. In the larger scheme of things, this is likely true, but unfortunately, everything can't be explained in a thirty-second window.

Sound Bites

The few sentences you use to describe your work should be brief yet powerful. Where we often see people go wrong with their elevator pitch, aside from rambling, is that they wind up overusing jargon that perhaps only people within their company or who are knee-deep in the business understand. Your consumer or the decision maker may not necessarily need to know your jargon to make a purchase. They simply want to believe in what you're saying. Belief is correlated with the human factor that we talked about earlier. It taps into the emotion associated with your stored memories. Belief creates inspiration, and when someone believes your company can inspire, then you likely just opened the door for a brand-new customer.

Another way people go wrong is that they wind up listing off their services as if they were menu items. Imagine going to dinner, and the waiter spends two minutes rattling off the specials for the day, which they spent the whole day memorizing, only to realize at the end that you weren't actually paying attention. The waiter went too fast and was so monotone that you have to ask them to repeat the first item again, oh, and the last one, and what was that one in the middle again? And after all that, you say, "You know what? Do you mind telling them to me again one more time?"

When creating sound bites about your company, think of them as your key message points. If someone were to walk away from a conversation with you, what are the three to four most important things you would want them to have taken from the interaction, without going into full-detail descriptions? For example, a client we worked with created a fintech platform that allowed non-accredited investors to invest in startup companies. For press purposes, we would pitch the company to the media, and the first talking point would be based around the company's innovation and the effect/solution they have for people. We would say, "The company is democratizing investing so everyday people like you and me can invest as little as $10 in startup companies before they become the next Uber or Twitter of the world with their own IPOs."

The problem that was being solved was that unless you were an investor at a venture capital investment firm, or the company was public and available on the stock market for purchase, everyday people didn't have the capability or availability to invest in startup companies.

Inflection

Have you ever heard the phrase "It's not what you say; it's how you say it"? Well, in business, that applies to everything you do. Inflection is the change in your tone of voice as you speak and, in the case of business, as you present.

Results from a study at the University of Chicago show the average human ear can distinguish 1,378 noticeable differences in tone, but the average human eye can distinguish only 150 hues of color. So our hearing is almost ten times more sensitive than our eyesight. Research also shows that *how* you say something is five times more important than *what* you actually say.[2]

Upward inflection, also known as upspeak, is the change of your pitch from lower to higher within the vowel, usually toward the end of a sentence. This type of inflection generally indicates a question, insincerity, surprise, or even suspense. This is not suited for all settings, however. For instance, you don't want to use this when sharing statistics or during negotiations. Try saying these words while *raising* your pitch at the end: Really? No way! Yes!

Downward inflection is the opposite. It is the change of your pitch from higher to lower. It is often associated with confidence and power, so you will want to use this when you are aiming to close a deal, presenting a resolution to a problem, or even stating a statistic. Try saying these words while *lowering* your pitch at the end: Done. Later. No.

Level inflection is when there is no change to the pitch. This can insinuate disinterest and indecisiveness. Try saying these words without changing your tone: Okay. Maybe. Fine.

Changing the tone of your voice can help create excitement, ignite belief, and also create a lasting impression for the person hearing it. You also want to be cautious when using inflections, because you don't want to upspeak the entire conversation during business calls. Upspeak, as well as downward and level inflection, need to be used strategically and saved for the right moments. When used properly, you will notice the power inflection holds and the belief it creates in your listener.

STYLES OF COMMUNICATION

Think back to a time you were in a heated discussion with a client. You were trying to explain a situation to them, and they were so caught up in being mad that you felt you weren't being heard, and they weren't understanding your process or reasoning. This tension is caused by a breakdown of communication. Everyone has a different communication style, so when you get into a situation with someone who has a completely opposite style, the two of you wind up not hearing each other, which likely results in you both walking away unhappy with each other.

Communicating with outside people, be it a customer or a media person, is important to your public relations strategy, because it will affect how an outsider perceives you and your company. Recognizing a person's communication style will help avoid potential conflict, as you will be able to adapt or rephrase sentences or questions to help that person process the information better. Understanding the way a passive person thinks or how an aggressive person may respond will increase the likelihood of a successful conversation. So, let's take a look at the four styles of communication so you can be better prepared the next time you meet with customers or the media.

The Four Styles of Communication

- *Passive:* A person who is passive has difficulty expressing their feelings, which can cause misunderstandings or built-up anger. They also have difficulty saying no. Passive people are "go with the flow" and are considered safer to speak with when conflict arises, because they will do their best to avoid conflict and likely won't lash back. You can recognize a passive person if they have difficulty making eye contact, have poor posture, go with the flow, and have trouble saying no.

- *Aggressive:* Someone who is aggressive tends to come across as a very strong personality, which is why they are inclined to be in more leadership roles but are seen more as bosses than leaders. They have a loud, dominating voice that can be intimidating or somewhat threatening to others. You can recognize an aggressive person when they are dominating a conversation. They also tend to issue orders, criticize, interrupt others, point and glare intently, and come across to others as making it all about them.

- *Passive-aggressive:* This is a person who appears passive on the surface level but, in reality, struggles with expressing their emotions directly. There tends to be hidden resentment that comes through in very subtle and indirect ways. Someone who is passive-aggressive may not confront you directly, but they may mumble a complaint or two under their breath. They may appear cooperative but be thinking otherwise. You can recognize a passive-aggressive person when they have difficulty expressing their feelings. Their words or facial expressions don't align with their actions, and they may use the "silent treatment" or even spread rumors behind other people's backs.

- *Assertive:* Thought of as the most effective and healthy way to communicate, assertive people are less overbearing and are more welcoming to an open and honest dialogue or discussion. Someone who is assertive considers the needs of others while also being self-aware enough to express their own needs and feelings. They often use statements that begin with "I." For example, "I understand you need help, and I would like to help you" or "Even if we don't agree, I respect your opinion." You can recognize an assertive person when they encourage a fair conversation and can confidently express their personal desires and needs while still respecting yours. Assertive people also maintain good eye contact and are able to say no.

Depending on the person you are speaking with and the situation you are in, you can tailor your message to the other person's communication style to ensure the conversation goes smoothly. For instance, when communicating with someone who is passive, you can expect them to have difficulty saying no up front. If you are looking for an honest answer from someone who is passive, ask direct questions and reassure the person that you appreciate their honest feedback. If you are dealing with someone who is aggressive, however, it's best not to mirror their aggression. That may only make the situation worse. Instead, stay calm and logical. Someone who is aggressive may get frustrated and become louder if they feel as if you aren't listening or they aren't being heard, so it is good to share with them that you hear and understand their feelings. You can even paraphrase key points they are trying to convey.

The good thing about communication styles is that they can easily be taught. When you are the one leading the conversation and you feel yourself falling too much into the aggressive territory, for example, you can pull yourself back by pausing to hear what the other person has to say. Then you can respond using an "I" statement. The important thing is to be mindful of your communication style in that moment, the communication style of the person on the receiving end, and how you can adjust what you are saying so your message is best received.

EFFECTIVE COMMUNICATION

The four styles of communication can be applied to all communication channels and are applicable to all employees, not just those in leadership roles. Take, for instance, a team of customer service representatives who are engaging with those sometimes-unhappy customers. How the representatives respond will decide if a customer continues to support your company or if they move to a competitor, or even tell their friends about the bad customer service they had. "You can't always please everyone" is said for a reason—because it's true—but how you respond to someone's negative feedback will be key in changing their mind.

The four styles of communication come into play during these types of interactions, because if a customer rep is on a phone call, then the importance of tone is amplified. The 7 percent rule by Albert Mehrabian concludes that communication is made up of three parts. Seven percent is the actual words you use, 38 percent is the tone of your delivery, and 55 percent is the body language used to accompany your words.[3] If you are on a phone call, then you are already missing 55 percent of the communication process. The outcome of the call rests on the words and the delivery. In essence, the tone of your customer service rep represents the tone of your company, which is why it is important to combine the human factor with the four styles of communication. Each customer communicates differently, so your reps conveying the human factor in their communication style will help alleviate negative feelings the customer is expressing. How the customer is treated is how they will perceive the brand moving forward. So remember to cater your communications to the communication style of the person you are interacting with.

In 2018 a group of passengers embarked on a fifteen-day cruise, only to realize once they left the port that the very cruise ship they were on was under construction. Instead of hearing the tranquil sounds of the sea, passengers experienced sounds of heavy hammers and grinders, and we aren't talking standard maintenance. There was grinding and sanding, so much so that some passengers were sent to the ship's infirmary for breathing problems, which the ship later charged them for.

Over five hundred passengers were upset they had spent thousands of dollars for an experience that turned out to be subpar. They even held a meeting to confront the captain with the complaints. The captain eventually stormed out. Soon after, the news stations caught wind of this, and the cruise ship issued a generic statement that they continuously aim to offer the best vacation experience for all their guests and that they acknowledge some customers may have experienced some inconvenience. The statement concluded that guests had been offered a 25 percent discount on their next booking, which was valid for only one year. There was no apology, and the cruise line didn't take a moment to recognize the individuals or their feelings of disappointment after having such a bad experience on their ship. The human factor would have considered how much money some families had to save to even take a fifteen-day vacation and how they chose that particular ship to embark on a potentially once-in-a-lifetime experience.

If the cruise line had training in place, the captain would have known how to best communicate with the passengers on the ship. Storming out of the meeting was likely a result of him feeling frustrated that the cruise line put him in a situation that required him to respond to such a large group of people. He may have been worried that his job would be affected if he said too much. He may have even realized it was an unfair situation for the passengers and that the cruise line was wrong for allowing people to board a ship that was undergoing major repairs. Analyzing the human factor in this situation and using the four styles of communication would have helped alleviate a bad situation. Instead, it is unlikely those passengers took that discounted voucher. It is more likely they told their friends about the nightmare experience they had, and they may even have found a few websites where they could post bad reviews.

Communication is key in every situation. When dealing with large groups of people, it's important to bear in mind that you are dealing with all four communication styles, and how you respond should be highly sufficient for a majority of the group, if not all of it. It's important for the group to feel heard and understood while your company takes action to make the scenario better for all.

❝❝ Innovation Station ❞❞

Verbal storytelling is different from the written word, because you're only given a short window to present your case and make a good first impression. When your story is available in written form, whoever is sitting down to read it may have the time to dig deeper and read up in greater length. But when you are telling your story in person, it needs to be concise yet hit all of the key points to entice the listener to take action and learn more. As TOMS founder Blake Mycoskie once said, "I realized the importance of having a story today is what really separates companies. People don't just wear our shoes, they tell our story."[4]

When you are detailing your story, start with the shortened version that can be given during any conversation, even one that is a casual encounter at the grocery store. If the person has time and they are genuinely interested in what you are telling them, they can ask follow-up questions or schedule some time with you to learn more later. You always want to make sure that your innovation is clear; the person should be able to share the conversation with another potential customer and include your story's characters, the setting, the plot, the conflict, and the resolution you offer.

With some practice, you'll be making connections while in the coffee line and whizzing through your next networking event!

CHAPTER 6

The Competitor Landscape

A horse never runs so fast as when he has other
horses to catch up and outpace.

—OVID, *The Love Books of Ovid*

When innovators come to us with their startup company, one of the main reasons they are looking to hire a PR firm is because they are the first of their kind, and they want to make sure the world knows that before someone else claims to be. Often companies that didn't implement a PR strategy from the beginning come to us, and now they are playing catch-up, because a competitor that they feel doesn't offer as great a product or service is getting all the market coverage in the media. Press coverage not only increases credibility but also helps you gain greater market share by allowing you to own the conversation.

Think of a large group of friends. There's Tom, who is the reserved person known for being a good listener and doesn't like conflict. There's Janet, who has a lot to say but doesn't know how to interrupt to share it. There's Allen, the "I agree" person who is part of the conversation but doesn't really share his own opinion. Then there's Allie, who is the alpha of the group and leads the conversation. Janet may have a topic to discuss that she is an expert in, but because she isn't loud enough, her voice remains silenced, and the group may never know what she is thinking. Allie, on the other hand, confidently expresses herself, and the group automatically believes her perspective on the subject, whether her stories are credible or not. The same scenario goes for brands. If a brand is louder and more vocal about their respective industry, it's more likely someone in that field will think of them first and make them the go-to source for more information. It can be frustrating when potential customers think of your competitor first, even though you offer a better product or service. As you build out your PR strategy, a review of your online presence in comparison to your competitors will help lay the foundation for your work moving forward.

DEFINING A COMPETITOR

In terms of media coverage, it's important to know both your direct and indirect competitors. A direct competitor offers the *same* product or service to the same market share as you, whereas an indirect competitor offers a *different* product or service also to the same market share. List out the companies that fall into each category. Aside from sizing up your competition, the reason we want to focus on competitors as part of the public relations strategy is so we can see what the media has to say about them, who has covered them, and how that can be leveraged for your brand. It essentially assesses what the media's appetite is for covering a topic relevant to your business.

When you are building out your list of competitors, a suggested format is Excel, with each company having their own worksheet. Start by listing out the company name, their social media handles, and how many followers or likes they have on each of their social media channels. Also include when the company was started, so you can gauge how long they've been working on their brand image. This will help you size up the competition and let you know how much you'll need to obtain to reach that level or, as is always the goal, to go above and beyond.

Underneath the company snapshot you've created, start a grid that has these headings, as shown in Table 6.1: Date, Media outlet, Title of article, Writer, and Notes. After you do this, you are ready to start your research. Head over to Google and go to the News section. Type in the company name with quotation marks around it and then different variations of it. For instance, if we were researching "Nike," we could also try "Nike shoes," "Nike corporate," "Nike CEO," and so on. Whatever you want to research about the company, try adding that as an extension of your search. A company like Nike will have thousands of results, but for smaller companies, the number will be manageable enough to include them all in the worksheet.

List them out in chronological order and make note of who wrote the article, the title, and how the company was featured. Note the angle of the article and how the company was included within that angle. This information will be helpful later as you examine it and ask yourself, "What is the media's perception of this brand?" And then, "How do I want my startup to be perceived similarly or differently?" It's important to know what makes your startup innovative so you can set yourself apart from your competitors and do what no one else is doing.

Table 6.1: Competitor analysis chart

Date	Media outlet	Title of article	Writer	Notes
November 20, 2020	*Forbes*	"How to Humanize the Public Relations Experience"	Jenna Guarneri	Writer (yes, me!) discussed connecting with the client, the media, and employees. Did not include any expert voice quotes.

Aside from researching your competitors, you can also look at aspirational brands. Who do you admire in terms of their positive reputation, and who has received a constant flow of media coverage? You can do this for yourself as a spokesperson of the company. For instance, we worked with a founder of a franchise company, and when assessing his personal PR strategy, we looked not only at the indirect and direct competitors but also at the public profiles of well-known spokespeople. This helped us gain a better understanding of how long they took to attain such an image, how they are featured in the media, and how a franchise could be on the same level as these household names. While you research competitors and other aspirational brands, you can also start a running document of past press and social media statistics for yourself, too. This will help you keep track of what you've achieved and how that compares to where you need to be.

THE PRESS

When you are researching your competitors, you will want to understand the caliber of the media outlet they are featured in, as well as the quality of the feature itself. But first, you'll need a better understanding of the media landscape, a foundation in the terminology often used, and knowledge of how those words can be interchanged. For instance, a member of the press can be a reporter, journalist, writer, editor, and so on. Companies or individuals can obtain *press coverage* or *media coverage*, and that coverage can also be referred to as *features*. Those features can be turned into *press clippings*, which can then be added to a *press kit*. Also, a public relations professional can also be known as a *publicist*.

Media Features

The golden ticket of media coverage is a *feature* story devoted entirely to you, a "valentine" if you will. There are quotes from you or your spokesperson, and there are photos of you in action or of the company, whether it's of the employees or the products. All of the brand's core message points are included, as well as hyperlinks back to the company website. Your innovation is fully explained, as well as your key differentiators from anything else on the market. It's almost as if you wrote it yourself or took out an advertisement. The information included is exactly what you want people's takeaway to be.

It's important to keep in mind that while this is always the biggest and best type of media placement, this is not always attainable. Unless you want to take on the cost associated with an advertisement, it is entirely up to the reporter how they want to present the story and up to their team how long or short they can make the story. It is often said that public relations is based on relationships. In this instance, that means rapport and etiquette. It would be considered in poor taste to request a story be of a certain size or length. So, if a reporter is interested in writing a story about your brand, the best way to achieve this would be to supply them with as much information as possible, without putting in any special requests like size or placement.

Another type of media feature is a media *mention*—that is, the story is devoted to a specific topic or trend, and you're mentioned briefly within that story. These aren't the biggest wins for a publicist, because clients always want the big feature story, but they are important to the overall brand. A mention means you are a part of a conversation. It shows that a reporter thought of you and deemed it necessary to include you. Would you like your competitors mentioned and you not at all? Much better if the reporter mentioned you and not your competitor. That's a win in and of itself. The message that this type of mention conveys is that you are being recognized and that you are a part of the conversation.

Alternatively, a *roundup story* highlights a select group of people or companies and includes brief information on each. An example is when you are looking online for the best of a product—let's say an air fryer. You'll see various stories for the "Ten Best Air Fryers" or the "Best Air Fryers under $100," and after you click the link, you'll scroll through to see an image alongside the name of the brand, the price, a short description of what makes this air fryer unique, and a link to the company's website for purchase. The same can be done for service companies and brands that don't sell a direct-to-consumer product. It also doesn't have to be shown as a list. It can be structured as a written story.

Media Outlet Categories

A media outlet is the platform where your press feature lives. There are thousands upon thousands of media outlets in existence. Knowing the category of media is important as you draft pitches and target reporters, so you can create a targeted list of media outlets for your PR strategy. What a reporter of a daily local newspaper is looking for in a story will be different from an editor of a national monthly magazine, so you will need to tailor your message and craft the proper story angle around it. Following are the various categories of media that can be tailored to both national and regional (local) media outlets.

Print Publications

Print publications are the media we know to be printed and physically held in our hands. These publications are broken down into newspapers and magazines.

Newspapers: Daily and weekly newspapers are great for sharing timely announcements and events, expressing issues or concerns, and covering breaking news items. Something that is "breaking news" requires instantaneous coverage, which is why daily newspapers have historically worked so well with getting this news out. Breaking news isn't a company announcement or anything relevant only to you. For something to be considered breaking news, it has to be highly important to a large group of people. A worldwide pandemic is an example, as is new legislation or laws that would affect a large group of people, such as speed cameras or the legalization of cannabis.

As you may already be familiar with from your local newspaper, newspapers generally have set sections and can include anything from general news, business, lifestyle, food, and features, to op-eds (opinion pieces), letters to the editor, politics, and events. Many newspapers are local, but there are a handful of select newspapers that you can find distributed across the United States, such as *The Wall Street Journal*, *The New York Times*, *USA Today*, and occasionally *The New York Post*, *The Washington Post*, and other metro city newspapers.

Magazines: Issued either weekly, monthly, bimonthly, or quarterly, and sometimes as a special edition, magazines can often be referred to as *glossies*, because of the shine the covers are known to have. Aside from weekly magazines, which are tied to timely news (think of the celebrity weekly magazines that share the latest in celebrity gossip), each issue of a magazine typically has a theme.

These themes are announced before the calendar year within the magazine's media kit. The media kit can be found on the magazine's website, or you can request it from the publisher, whose contact information you can find online.

As you review the themes, you may notice one that suits your company and your story better than others. This will help you tailor your pitch to the reporters to be specific and suitable to the issue's theme, which increases the chances of your story being included. Additionally, each magazine has regular columns and features that appear in every issue. The cover story is always different, and that generally introduces the theme itself, but the regular columns are standard, so you can expect the same writers for those in each issue. If you review five to eight past issues of the magazine you are targeting, you can find patterns and trends that will help you develop a story to best target those readers.

Broadcast Media

Broadcast media sends electronic signals with audio or video content to the masses.

Television: One of the hardest media categories to break into, television takes a much different level of skill from a spokesperson than a phone interview or an email Q&A. The more popular a television show is, the leerier a producer is of putting a spokesperson on the air. The worst thing as a viewer is watching an interview with someone who is so nervous that they stammer, respond in short sentences, and look like a deer in the headlights. If you are looking to be a guest on the number-one national morning show in the United States or on a serious national business channel, then you need to have examples of past video segments you've appeared on as evidence of your ease and comfort in front of a camera. This sounds like a chicken-before-the-egg type of situation, because how do you become experienced without being given your first opportunity?

The strategy we've implemented in the past for our clients who had no prior television experience was starting with regional television. The bar for entry is much lower, so long as you have a tie to that regional market. For companies that have a service or product that isn't local but is available online and nationwide, I start by looking at where the company is based or even where the founders are based. New York and Los Angeles are the most difficult regional television markets, because they compete with the national television networks; but for all the cities in between, the regional markets are generally very open to television interviews, so long as you have a reason for that specific market to care about your product and your company on a personal level.

Sometimes you can even have a spokesperson visit the town and create a small event where the general public can meet that person, and you can promote the event on the regional morning show. If the founder of the company lives within the regional market, even better. Then you can promote the brand as being developed by "one of its own." Locals love supporting other locals.

Insider Tips and Tricks

Joelle Garguilo, an Emmy Award–winning reporter and producer and cofounder of Make Media Moves, shared some of her tips for landing a TV placement as an expert, even without having prior television experience.[1] Joelle explained that it used to be industry standard for potential guests on a program to show similar press as examples in order to be considered. The obstacle, though, was that if you didn't have press, then how would you get press?

Joelle shared that in today's digital age, those types of obstacles no longer exist, and the best thing anyone can do is record themselves on their phone. Taking out a phone and talking to a screen can be a challenge for some people, but if you can do so in a natural way, it shows a reporter like Joelle that you would be just as comfortable on television. Also, consistently posting to your social media channels is now a modern version of the traditional *sizzle reel*, which refers to a video compilation of your top video interviews spliced together. The sizzle reel was what you traditionally presented to reporters for consideration to be a guest on their program. It would show them that you were comfortable on camera and could hold a conversation naturally.

When Joelle looks at someone's social media channels, she wants to see that you have personality and that you can provide a consistent and clear message. "It used to be that in order to be considered an expert, you needed to have a book or something large scale, but in today's world, anyone with social media can position themselves to be considered an expert."

But to be *good* at being an expert on social media, you need to have a "clear vision of what it is that you're trying to do. If you want to be an expert in the field of beauty, then show me videos filled with beauty tips," Joelle explains. "Social media is the new résumé."

As a producer, whenever she books someone on a show or interviews them for a segment, she is putting her reputation on the line for that person, so she wants to make sure that they can, in fact, deliver a great segment. Now, with social media as a touchpoint, Joelle can almost instantaneously check someone's camera-ready skills. Having that video content on your page is proof you are an authority in your space and can handle camera interviews.

In addition to using social media as leverage for being on television, Joelle explains that it's equally important to understand

continued

why "you want to be on this particular television show. You can't just be on the show for the sake of being on it. Do your homework. Watch the show. If you are asking a reporter or producer to take a moment to consider your pitch, then make sure the topic you want to discuss is one that aligns with the format of the show. You're asking somebody to take their time to go through it and try to make sense of it for their show, so why don't you do the homework for them and present it in a way that makes sense for them? A little homework goes a long way, because reporters and producers are constantly in search of new concepts for the show."

Radio: This was previously viewed as a primary source of news and entertainment in the early 1950s, before the arrival of television. It was truly the first form of mass communication that allowed broadcasters to reach millions of people instantly. AM and FM radio are known for the differences in sound quality, as FM uses a higher-frequency range, as well as the differences in content featured on each. FM has become most associated with music, while AM is more talk radio and includes the latest in traffic, weather, and sports. While the market for news has become quite competitive since the inception of radio, it is still a daily go-to source for many, especially commuters during their morning and evening drives home. FM radio tends to feature guests of a celebrity status, but they do on occasion make announcements for events and happenings in the area, whereas AM radio has more interview opportunities for local guests.

Digital Media

Digital media provides a forum for an endless amount of timely and instantaneous information.

Online components: These are the online versions of print publications. Because the Internet is so vast, it requires more content from the media outlet to stay relevant. Thus, the media outlet may generate more stories for online consumption than they do for print, which is why your story may be online but not necessarily in print. For the most part, though, most of the stories that go into print will automatically be put online. Aside from the reporters who write for the print publication (whose stories will also run online), there are reporters who are focused entirely on generating content for the magazine's website on a semi-regular basis (their stories will not appear in print).

Traditionally, print was the most coveted type of feature, but for startups, online coverage can sometimes produce far greater results. A handful of media outlets have rules about not including hyperlinks in a story, but for others, when a hyperlink is included, readers have the ability to click through to the company's website to either learn more, make a purchase, or inquire about services. This is also helpful for companies, because you can track the click-through rate back to your website and see the direct result of the media placement.

PR is not typically quantifiable, but this is one instance where you can find a hard number to represent a portion of the results achieved. I say portion because you can't fully measure the results of PR, since PR is a long-term strategy that affects perception. PR is not meant to create instantaneous results, so while I don't suggest relying on click-through rates or sales from one media placement, it helps you gauge how well your overall strategy is working.

Websites: Standalone pages do not have a print component and operate similar to that of a magazine, with teams of editors and reporters. The main difference is the amount of content websites have to produce on a daily basis. A writer can have several stories to write in one day, and those can go up on the website as quickly as the end of the day, whereas magazines have a much longer lead time and can take months to publish the final article. Online reporters don't have a lot of time in between their deadlines, so if they are working on a story and request a quote or interview, make sure to respond quickly and adhere to their scheduling. Again, etiquette and rapport are important in public relations, so don't make it about your scheduling. If a reporter gives you times of availability, take what they give you. No one likes dealing with the back-and-forth that comes with scheduling. If you make scheduling difficult, there's a strong chance the reporter may go MIA because they went with someone more accommodating than you.

Podcasts: Long-form auditory experiences, podcasts commonly feature guests discussing their background, how they got started, and things like their theories and platform. Podcasts have more flexibility in terms of content, because they don't have a radio station backing them and, therefore, no one to answer to in terms of scripts, advertisers, and sound levels. When someone develops a podcast, they upload it directly to their chosen platform, and it's ready for listening. Podcasts are typically hosted on iTunes, Spotify, Stitcher, and RadioPublic. There's usually a theme behind the podcast, and not all podcasts feature guests, so it's important to review the podcast's past shows for trends and relevancy.

Types of Media Outlets

Along with the different media categories, media can be divided by topic. *Trade publications* cover specific industries or niche categories.

For example, while a liquor brand can appeal to everyday consumers and appear in mainstream news, there are media outlets (or trades) that are devoted solely to covering the latest liquor product launches, as well as company news and updates. Trade publications help increase a brand's credibility and recognition. Your startup needs to be recognized among industry peers and professionals as a competitive leader before it can be recognized as such by people not in your space.

We are all familiar with the media outlets that are sold near the checkout lines of the supermarket. These are the mainstream media that generally fall into the category of *national consumer* and are targeted toward the general public. They cover a series of topics to reach the appeal of a wide audience. They usually have a high readership rate and are popular among advertisers. Your favorite health and fitness publications or go-to car resources all fit into this category. *Lifestyle publications* is another term that can be used to describe your favorite publications covering food, home and design, travel, and anything that can appeal to you in your day-to-day personal life.

Business media is one type of media that is often appealing to startups and businesses alike. While your product or service may not appeal to the national consumer press, business media coverage allows an opportunity for niche businesses to obtain press outside of their usual trade media coverage. Because business media reaches a wide audience, there is a good chance the C-suite executives within your niche category are reading it. This means business media can help increase brand visibility among your competitors and increase potential investor interest. You may even recruit talented individuals for your team. National business publications are read by discerning individuals, and the content developed is highly researched. Therefore, you can expect high-quality stories that have the potential to take a company to the next level.

❦❦ Innovation Station ❦❦

The media world, in and of itself, is competitive, so doing your due diligence in advance will help you successfully navigate it. Whether you are the first company of your kind or not, others will always be vying for the same type of media coverage as you. When it comes to the news, there will always be competition. Being prepared and doing the prep work beforehand will help you achieve results in the media for your company while simultaneously increasing your brand recognition.

Once you familiarize yourself with your competitors, the media world, and how your competitors are featured within the world of media, you have officially laid the foundation for your PR strategy. You can take the competitor analysis you created, similar to the sample in Table 6.1, and use it for your goal setting, or what I often refer to as "Affect and Project." This entails taking what your competitors produce with their own media coverage and using it to project your own goals and differentiators.

To begin your competitor analysis, ask yourself:

- How are my competitors affecting their audience through the media?

- How am I offering something different?
- Are they engaging with their audience on a human level?
- If not, how can I improve that for my audience?

{ **Part III** }

LAUNCH

CHAPTER 7

Strategy Development

Hope is not a strategy.

—RICK PAGE, *Hope Is Not a Strategy*

Analyzing our work as publicists as compared to that of a "desk job" has always been a common discussion among our team. Desk work often consists of projects that have a clear start and finish. When the person is done with the project, they can push that work aside and not look back at it. Oh, how nice it must be to be satisfied with a completed project. Naturally, this isn't the case for all desk jobs, but we use it as a point of reference to show that the job of a publicist is the complete opposite.

Our projects are never done, because public relations is a long-term strategy. Our job consists of multiple small tasks, and each task works toward a bigger task or a bigger goal. It's like a chipper effect:

We chip away one media hit at a time to consistently push toward getting the next big story, which will hopefully be larger in size and in an even more renowned media outlet. But to get there, you need to understand the strategy and the bigger goals that you want to achieve.

When potential new clients come to me, for example, I can always tell who understands public relations and who does not. This is primarily based on the first phone conversation. The people who come to us and say they have an announcement to make next week and think it's "perfect for *The Wall Street Journal*" don't understand the PR process. If they did, they would know that *The Wall Street Journal* is pitched daily by hundreds of people, and guess what? Those people also think their announcement is big enough for the *WSJ* to write about them.

It's very rare that a major publication will pick up a story that quickly, especially without having ever seen the company's or person's name before. One story can take weeks to pitch out, and it's not always the top media outlet or even your first choice that will pick up the story. That's why if a company comes to us requesting to be featured in a specific top-tier media outlet, and they expect it in a short window of time, they likely won't be our client. They don't understand the time and strategy needed to be effective in the public relations process.

Have you ever been in bumper-to-bumper traffic, and you can't figure out what the cause of the nightmare is because you're so far back in line that you can't see anything? Then, forty-five minutes later, you get closer to the point of madness, and you notice everyone has their right blinker on and is trying to get over. People are honking, and no one is following the rules of the white dotted lines. Naturally, everyone is worried about themselves and getting to where they have to be.

Slowly but surely, you inch your way over to the right, like everyone around you. As soon as you get in the far-right lane and get through the mass of cars, you finally can tap on the gas to give it a little go. Ah, the sigh of relief as you start to feel the open road ahead of you! As you start to drive, you look over and realize that all three lanes on the far left are closed off for construction. You were basically in one big funnel consisting of four lanes merging into one. How crazy! But that's exactly what it's like when people pitch reporters.

This may seem like a drastic example to make a point, but it's the same thing in PR when people pitch to the same media source: one big funnel! Dozens, if not hundreds, of people pitch a single reporter on any given day, especially if it's a major media outlet. The reporters have to sort through their emails and, like the example of the cars, create a funneling system that decides which emails will go to the next step.

That's why you have to ensure what you're pitching is quality information, because when the reporter does get to your email, you want them to stop and realize it's not like every other pitch they received that day. On top of that, a pitch requires strategic follow-ups to ensure the reporter didn't accidentally glance over your email the first time. And that's why we can't just hit Send on an email and be done. Media relations consists of many strategic tactics spread out over a long period of time.

PR STRATEGIZING

Your PR strategy can be broken down into two categories: short- and long-term. We look at the two separately because they require different approach tactics. They each depend on different categories of media, which have different lead times. Think of the traditional national print magazine you see at your local bookstore, which releases a new issue each month. This is considered a *long-lead publication*, because those editorial teams work on that month's issue four to six months in advance. The type of content featured in a national magazine is different from that in a local newspaper, which is considered a *short-lead publication*.

You determine your strategy based on your goals. Are you looking to obtain a lot of press in a short window? If so, you'll want to focus on a short-term approach. Short-lead publications typically turn out content quicker, so they're constantly looking for more stories and scheduling more interviews. If you're looking for a press placement with a highly read and regarded media outlet, then you need a long-term strategy for securing the feature, which requires the time needed to craft the proper story and to target, pitch, and follow up with the proper reporter for it.

Long-Term Strategy

Are you opening a new store, and its grand opening to the public is set for four months from now? Are you raising money from investors, and you expect to close the round of funding by quarter one of next year? Or how about that acquisition deal you're working on that's expected to be finalized and ready for an announcement in five months? Whatever your big announcement is, it should be listed within your long-term strategy. These are actual events/happenings that can be pegged to a day and time on the calendar and are more than three months from now.

The benefit to establishing a long-term strategy is that you are building a foundational relationship with reporters to reinforce key brand messaging while increasing brand recognition among these key individuals. This way, when you do have a project or announcement to share with that person a few months from now, they aren't hearing from you for the very first time. You have already spoken to the person, and maybe you've even pitched them. The reporters already have a built-in interest in what you are doing.

Reporters usually also have a long list of articles they're assigned from their superiors, so any articles they decide to take on from a pitch they received gets added to their pile. You are on the reporters' time, so you can't bring them a story last minute and expect them to have the bandwidth to take it on, research it, do the interviews needed, and issue the article the day and time you want it out. No way would a writer ever do that! And really, why should they? Do you like when someone tells you how and when to do your job?

The types of press angles that should be incorporated into a long-term strategy include announcements, events, launches of new services or products, the opening of a new store, acquisitions or partnerships, and fundraising efforts, among many others. Think of it this way: If it takes months to make that announcement happen, that's considered a long-term press angle. Your PR strategy is built out in chronological order, so all those happenings become future press angles to work toward.

Aside from factoring in the long-term press angles, you should consider the type of media outlets that work on their own long-term scheduling. For media, it's called being a *long lead*. The long-lead publications plan their work far in advance because of the time it takes to publish and print the magazine. When pitching to these types of publications, you must factor in timing. If your story is set to occur in May, then reporters need to write a story by November for it to appear in a May issue.

You also have to factor in the length of a pitching cycle: giving reporters enough time to review a pitch, sending strategic follow-ups (not bombarding), and having to pitch other reporters when the one you initially hoped would write the story passes on it. The pitching and following-up cycle take weeks. Therefore, this also has to be taken into consideration.

When emailing reporters, you'll want to make sure you have the specifics of the announcement. You can't just pitch someone with "really exciting news" that you'll share once it's "finalized." You've just wasted a pitch by doing so. Don't send out any pitches unless you have all the information ready to share, including professional photos. You'll also need to give you and your team time to prep the proper messaging and assets before you even start pitching.

Short-Term Strategy

While PR requires a long-term strategy to continuously build good-will, create a positive reputation, and enhance brand awareness, there are instances when a short-term strategy can be incorporated into your larger strategy. As the phrase suggests, the short-term strategy consists of things happening today, tomorrow, and the next day, even within the current month. While you're waiting for your long-term press to run, a short-term press strategy will produce smaller press placements in the days, weeks, and months leading up to your long-term press strategy.

Eventually your short-term strategy will meet up with your long-term strategy. The goal is to have press placements continuously running. This way, if someone doesn't read the national magazine you will be featured in three months from now, they can catch you in the local newspaper tomorrow. Or if they see you in the newspaper *and* in the national magazine later, you are beginning the process of creating strategic brand recognition.

Short-term press strategies don't require a level of planning as elaborate as the long-term strategies. That's simply because the story angles generated aren't as complex. Take, for instance, the PR tactic called *newsjacking*, which is a term first coined by David Meerman Scott in 2011. Newsjacking is when brands take what's happening in the current news cycles and piggyback off of it for their own content. Because it's so timely, newsjacking has the potential to create immediate impact, but it needs to be handled properly and carefully. Breaking news can be geared toward the general public, like a TV star mentioning the use of a certain type of product on a new episode of a top-watched television show. The next morning is timely, because you can go out with a pitch on how the show talked about using this type of product and you just so happen to offer the best dang version out there. Don't say you are the best, but give them the facts to figure it out for themselves!

Other examples of things that may be newsjacked are trends like the famous #IceBucketChallenge, which thrived in pop culture for a number of weeks, or big events like the Super Bowl. In 2013, the Super Bowl had a thirty-four-minute power outage, and almost instantaneously Oreo went out with a clever Tweet, saying, "Power out? No problem." Oreo paired the Tweet with a photo of some Oreos faintly lit on a black background with the words, "You can still dunk in the dark."

But not all newsjacking has to deal with news relative to the general public. It can also pertain to newly released laws and regulations that are more specific to your industry. For instance, are you a drone company, and the Federal Aviation Administration (FAA) has just issued a new regulation in relation to drone delivery? A pitch to the reporters covering drones can pertain to the product you offer, or you can pitch the reporters that cover the FAA, offering expert advice from a thought leader, your founder, or perhaps a spokesperson going on record discussing the new law and how it directly pertains to your industry.

The following are some keys to newsjacking:

- Don't wait for the story to become "old news."

- Aim to get your story out instantly. If that's not possible, don't wait longer than twenty-four hours.

- It's better to be among the first few responding rather than be lost in a sea of voices.

- Don't use controversy for your benefit. It will likely backfire.

- Don't try to leverage deaths or natural disasters.

- Make a clear connection between the news item and your brand.

- Be clear. There's no room for ambiguity and a potentially misconstrued opinion.

- Ensure the core values of the brand are shown in a positive way.

Of course, you don't want to newsjack just any story. The last thing you want is for your PR efforts to backfire and create a negative effect. If the news story is already negative, then there's no reason to voluntarily attach your name to that type of story. Let someone else do that. A celebrity's death or a natural disaster that has left hundreds without homes are examples of times when you do not want to be seen as generating content for your own benefit.

Don't make a story about you or try to infuse your brand into the message in a forceful way. In the case of a celebrity death, let the message be about the person. It will come across as being more genuine. When famed musician Prince died, the heartfelt messages and condolences from brands poured out over social media, including from the General Mills brand Cheerios, which issued a Tweet of "Rest in Peace" with a purple background and what they must've thought was clever, a Cheerio dotting the *i*. After receiving a stream of negative comments, Cheerios removed the Tweet and put out this statement: "As a Minnesota brand, Cheerios wanted to acknowledge the loss of a musical legend in our hometown. But we quickly decided that we didn't want the Tweet to be misinterpreted and removed it out of respect for Prince and those mourning."[1]

One of the biggest examples in history of news affecting the daily media cycles is COVID-19. As we just learned, brands using the news as a narrative for their content is considered newsjacking, but the COVID-19 pandemic is a completely unique instance. At the height of COVID-19, when cities first went into lockdown, news cycles were saturated with updates and breaking news coverage. COVID-19 became one of the most covered news topics in history and for the longest duration of time. No other news topics were as important, so naturally nothing else was being covered. And when I say nothing, I mean nothing. It is because of this that brands had a difficult time trying to stay relevant. They couldn't newsjack, because they ran the risk of receiving negative backlash by appearing tone deaf or for trying to capitalize on an unprecedented tragedy.

Cadbury is a popular chocolate often associated with the Easter holiday. During Easter of 2020, we were in the very early stages of quarantine and very much at the height of the pandemic and the height of fear among the entire nation. People didn't leave their homes, and families were separated to ensure safety for elders and those with pre-existing conditions. So, when Cadbury issued their Easter commercial showing a grandfather hiding Easter eggs around his apartment for his grandkids, the company received backlash, since the two generations were not supposed to spend time together.

Initially the brand's purpose, which was likely developed before the pandemic, was to flip the conversation and focus on the generosity of adults hiding the eggs, versus the traditional storyline of children hunting for the eggs. It also tapped into the brand ideal that entailed the spirit of generosity and bringing out that spirit during the Easter season. While the story was meant to be genuine and heartfelt, it was poor timing, and the company received numerous callouts on social media addressing the tone-deaf ad. Soon after, Cadbury pulled the ad and issued a statement of apology.

While the world was still navigating the early stages of the pandemic, Google took quick action to ban ads that even mentioned the coronavirus to prevent profiteering and misinformation. Working with our startup companies, we took a different approach. Instead of trying to put out traditional messages to promote our clients' brands, we stopped issuing any pitches relative to the brands and instead focused on thought leadership. Our pitches to the media focused on our clients' founders discussing topics such as how their teams were coping with the new virtual world, what they were doing to enhance employee culture, and how they were networking in a socially distanced world. All our stories gave tips to other business owners. There were actual takeaways that made the stories selfless and not promotional.

This type of content helped brands be a part of the conversation while avoiding backlash. Because each day of the pandemic brought new news, the media cycles were constantly changing how they covered the coronavirus. That is why the short-term PR strategies became so important. We constantly had to rework story angles and evaluate what message was being conveyed and how it aligned with the brands. As for the long-term strategies, they were put completely on hold. Businesses didn't know what the future would hold for them, and the media was focused on the world, which was focused on navigating a major pandemic.

Media Outlets

The short-lead media outlets most often associated with the short-term PR strategy are radio, podcasts, daily newspapers, weekly magazines, blogs, websites, and online components to national magazines. In contrast, the long-lead media outlets are aligned with the long-term PR strategy and include monthly, bimonthly, and quarterly print magazines. Keep in mind, print publications typically hit newsstands a month before the actual publication date, so if you go to the grocery store, you'll see the September issue on stands, even though it's still August.

Now, you may be wondering, could they be combined? The answer is yes. For instance, say it's January and you have a new product launch happening in October. You can pitch the long-lead media outlets as soon as you finalize the product materials and images, making sure to finish your pitch by March. You'll need to factor in the amount of time you need to send follow-up emails, send product sample mailings, and fulfill interview requests, which can take weeks, sometimes months. Once you get closer to that official October launch date, you can then work on short-lead media outlets. You would start this around August.

To help you determine which strategy is best for your PR goals, answer these questions:

- What is the timeline of your pitch angle? Is it tied to something that is more than six months out? Or is it relative to a pitch angle happening this month?

- What type of media outlets is your target audience consuming? Do they read the national print business magazines, or are they watching the news on television? Perhaps they are a mixture of both?

- What are your overall goals? Do you want a diverse press portfolio that includes a little bit of each media category?

- Is your company at a place for press to start writing large profiles on your brand? In case there is an increase in demand from the placement, can you properly accommodate and service those new customers?

ADDITIONAL PR TACTICS

PR is a process that incorporates many different elements. It's like opening up a new puzzle board and tossing all the pieces onto the floor. You don't know where to begin, so you keep grabbing new pieces and trying to fit them together, hoping for the right match. Frustrated, you eventually get your bearings and have a foundation of several pieces to start building around. The same can be said for PR. You try a few different approaches before the story sticks and gets picked up and written by a news outlet. The tactic you choose can then be incorporated into either your short- or long-term strategies.

The Evergreen Story Angle

Don't have a news hook or a formal announcement to make? No worries. That's actually very common. Naturally, as a business you can't always have a big announcement to make. The big announcements get plugged into your master PR strategy plan, and everything in between those announcements is called *evergreen press*. It's referred to as evergreen because there's no time stamp and the story doesn't expire, so it can be written about any day of the week and still be relevant. One of the reasons startup companies come to us for press is they are gearing up to do a round of fundraising, and the press will help create an added level of credibility when they are presenting to potential investors. During this time, the startup generally doesn't have an announcement for us to pitch out as a timely news hook. Instead, we create a time-sensitive story by focusing the pitch on the innovation. This way, the company can point to a problem that exists in the industry or in the world and show how their startup is solving that problem with a completely new approach.

Evergreen stories are usually in-depth feature stories about the company, tied to a trend relative to what's happening right now within the respective industry. These stories can take much longer to secure simply because there's no time sensitivity and they have no shelf life. Reporters are inundated with deadlines relative to breaking news announcements, deadlines given by their superiors, and pitches that have a time stamp, so something that is "evergreen" may get pushed to the bottom of their list.

However, how you present the evergreen story can change its time sensitivity. By tying your pitch to something currently being covered in the news, you make your story more timely. One example is to start with the news item and then present your founder as an expert voice who can discuss the topic and the respective industry. You can then discuss the founder's company and the innovation they offer. The availability of your product or service as a solution to the news item makes it timely. The evergreen pitch can be used during both your short- and long-term strategies. If you're pitching it paired with something happening in breaking news, then that is considered short-term. However, if you are focusing on the innovation of the offering and how it's changing an antiquated industry, then it is an ongoing pitching strategy and part of the long term.

Thought Leadership

Falling into the personal PR category, thought leadership is the sharing of knowledge by an individual to a large audience. Being a thought leader means you not only are known in your industry for being an expert but also hold great influence. Thought leaders have a platform with a loyal following and are widely regarded for the information they consistently share. By utilizing thought leadership in your PR strategy, you are maximizing the type of exposure you can get for your company.

When an expert is referenced as a source in an article, their credit line states, "Name, title, and company," so your company is always being referenced. For instance, if you are utilizing the founder of your company for thought leadership, the person is your company and vice versa. Since the company is the person, your company automatically benefits from the piece of press. In contrast, brand-specific PR describes the stories relative to the brand, which may not necessarily reference the founder.

Thought leadership can be in the form of attributions, profile stories, and byline articles (written by the thought leader). Thought leadership can also be shared daily via social media with thoughts on industry-relevant topics, tips and advice, and the latest news and updates. Thought leadership also creates an opportunity for a human connection among your network. People following and listening to your words get to know your perspective. Thought leaders are asked to speak at large conferences and be interviewed for various forms of media, like television and podcasts. If you keep up with it, you'll eventually be paid for all your public appearances. To develop your thought leadership requires a long-term commitment, a lot of energy, and an investment of your time.

❛❛ Innovation Station ❜❜

When developing your PR strategy, think about your goals and what the point of a media placement is for you. Not all companies want the national TV segment, because they may not be able to handle the influx of orders or requests that would come in from a media hit like that. Some companies just want a few media hits so they can work out the kinks of their business.

Some things to consider: Do you have a timely news hook that you can plan for months in advance? Or do you want to focus on an evergreen story about the innovation of your offering? Both would be a part of your long-term strategy, while things like breaking news and events happening later this month would fall within your short-term strategy. You can also maximize the type of exposure your company can obtain by incorporating both personal PR and brand-specific PR into your PR strategy. Have you considered thought leadership? If so, commit to sharing and developing content on a regular basis.

CHAPTER 8

Media Relations

Build relationships, don't collect them.

—REBEKAH RADICE, Twitter post, November 24, 2014

A fter realizing her car has exactly one month left on her lease, Lauren spends her Saturday shopping from one car dealership to the next. The salesperson at the first dealership walks over to her after he spots her walking around one of the vehicles on the show-room floor and asks, "What can I do for you today?" Lauren explains her car lease is about to end and that she is looking for an affordable vehicle. She doesn't use her car too often, since she takes the train to work each day, but she uses it on the weekends and occasionally on weeknights to run a few errands. They talk for a few minutes longer, and Lauren decides she wants a quote on a vehicle. The salesperson says, "Let me run the numbers, and I'll come back to you."

In the meantime, Lauren casually walks around the dealership and eventually comes across a lounge area, where she sits and grabs herself a bottle of water. She's waiting about twenty minutes, but no one bothers her. The salesperson comes back and gives her the price for a top-of-the-line version of the car she was looking at, with all the bells and whistles. Lauren is taken aback, since the price given is not what she considers affordable and, of course, not something that makes sense financially to her, since she uses her car sparingly. Embarrassed to admit it's above her price range, she tells the salesperson, "Great, I still have another month left, so I'll plan to come back in two weeks." In reality, though, Lauren walks out that door and heads into dealership number two.

The feel of this dealership is different as soon as Lauren walks in. When she opens the door, someone at the reception desk smiles and says, "Welcome! How can we help you today?" Lauren shares with the receptionist the same information that she did with the first dealership: Her lease is up, and she uses her car sparingly. The receptionist responds, "Great! I can have a salesperson help you shortly, if you want to get started looking around?" Lauren replies, "Sure." The receptionist follows up and says, "Can I get you a water or some coffee or tea in the meantime?" Lauren decides she can use some caffeine after the hours she's spent car shopping, so she says yes to some coffee. "How do you take it?" asks the receptionist. Lauren smiles. She likes the personal touches here.

Lauren sips her coffee as she walks around the first vehicle on the showroom floor. As she starts toward the second vehicle, a salesperson comes over to introduce himself. He continues, "I heard your car is going back and that you use your car somewhat sparingly?" Lauren nods and elaborates a little further on the details. The salesman continues, "Ballpark, what are you looking to spend each month on a lease?" Lauren shares her budget, and he says, "We definitely have something for you." He proceeds to show her two different vehicles and says, "We can work the numbers on that to be within budget, but it may not have all the bells and whistles."

Lauren says to herself, "He gets it!" He invites Lauren to sit at his desk while he does the math on his computer in front of her. He asks if Lauren wants a bagel while she waits. "Sure," she says. He calls reception, and the receptionist brings over the type of bagel Lauren asked for. After ten minutes, the salesman is done calculating the numbers on the first car, which is $50 below Lauren's original budget. *This is great. I'm definitely leaving here today with a new car*, Lauren thinks to herself. After the salesman works out the numbers on the second car, and the price is about the same as what Lauren initially budgeted, the salesman goes through all the features each car comes with. He even asks Lauren where she goes on weekends and what her hobbies are so he can get a better sense of how the vehicle will be used. After comparing her needs with the car features, she decides on vehicle number two, even though it is higher priced than the first option, albeit still within her original budget.

Lauren leaves the dealership feeling accomplished. She calls her dad on the way out to tell him all about the great deal she got and how easy the salesman made it for her. When Lauren goes to dinner the next weekend with her friends, she pulls up in her new vehicle, and her friends say, "Wow, great new car!" Lauren proceeds to tell them about her experience. The conversations continue as such throughout Lauren's "new car phase," and the dealership continues to be a part of the conversation as people ask her where she got her car. Months later, Lauren is on the phone talking to her friend, who mentions she has to get a new car soon. Lauren replies, "You have to check out the dealership I went to and ask for the salesman I worked with!"

A positive experience stems from the positive emotions felt by the person during an interaction. The second dealership offered much more to Lauren than the first dealership did. The receptionist and salesman treated her like a human being with basic needs. It was the small and simple things that added up into something larger. Not only did they offer her food and water, but the salesman also worked out the numbers in front of her. She felt she was a part of the process and that there was transparency. Lauren also felt understood after the salesman reiterated what she'd shared with the receptionist about not using her car often. He even inquired about her hobbies and how that would relate back to the car features. The salesman asked her up front about her budget, and because he delivered not only that but also an even better price, Lauren felt as if he was really on her side. The first dealership made Lauren feel as if the process was a transaction that mainly benefited the salesman, who was trying to make his sales goals for the month. The second dealership made Lauren feel as if she could trust them. Trust and respect are two key components in relationship building, as are acknowledgment and respect of each other's needs. Relationships are important not only in your personal life but in business, too.

Similar to Lauren, a media person wants to be treated like a human being with basic needs. By paying attention to a reporter's past work and getting to know them on a more personal level, you are creating a positive standout experience from your competitors, or in this case, other people pitching similar stories. Once you establish a relationship, you will have a reputation for being an easy person to work with.

IMPORTANCE OF RELATIONSHIPS

I'm sure somewhere along your startup journey you've heard the phrase "PR is all about relationships." I have to admit, if I ever heard someone saying this, I would instantly roll my eyes at them. That was mainly because of how it was being used; it was usually during a new business meeting, and the potential client didn't know very much about the PR industry, although they thought otherwise. They mainly assumed we would call up our "best friends" to write a big feature story, not taking into consideration whether they actually had a story worthy of a large feature or that, regardless of who we're friends with, a reporter has to respectfully report on what will appeal the most to their audience. Reporters are friends with a lot of publicists and a lot of business owners, so they can't do favors for everyone. Personal relationships can do nothing if there's no story to tell. For our purpose here, when we say, "PR is all about relationships," we are using it to describe our interactions with all facets of the media relations process: the client, our employees, and, of course, the media.

The client needs to trust their public relations team, and like anything else, this comes with time. Once the client onboards with an agency, it's the agency's job to deliver a great experience as soon as possible—that way, the client can feel confident in their investment.

For the employees of an agency, it's important to have strong relationships with their coworkers, because PR can really become a team effort. If someone has a lead they can share, they'll be able to make the proper introduction for another member of the team. It's about working together to ensure the client is receiving positive results, not about who selfishly owns and gets credit for the win. The relationships you have with media people are key, because they are the decision makers in whether your pitch will turn into a story or not. Media relationships are strategic and must be treated with sensitivity at all times to nurture the relationship over the long term.

Research

To lay the groundwork for building a relationship with a media person, you have to research. Knowing who you are pitching is absolutely key before hitting Send on any pitch emails. A specific person will write about your industry in a particular way, so you have to dig a little and go down a "rabbit hole" in terms of researching who that person is exactly. In journalism, the topic a reporter covers is known as their *beat*. The beat of a reporter covering the latest in the court and legal system is "crime," and the beat of a person covering the latest in football is "sports" with a specialization in football. The last thing a crime reporter wants to receive is a pitch about sports.

That's an obvious one, but you would be surprised at how often something like that actually does happen. And you don't want to be that person blind-pitching reporters and looking as if you don't know what you are doing. Not only does research help prevent blunders like this from happening, but it also shows the reporter that you did your homework. On top of wanting to look as though you know what you're doing, you also want to target key reporters so you can build relationships with them. Similar to what we discussed in the last chapter, having a reporter recognize your name repeatedly helps your company in the long term. Reporters are more prone to write about companies they are familiar with—companies they have watched scale and evolve.

Media Lists

As publicists, we are infamously known for our *media lists*, which are exactly what they sound like—lists of media people, consisting of their name, title, beat, email, sometimes a phone number, and links to past articles as examples. These lists are gold to a publicist, because they are a main resource for our day-to-day work. The value of one of these lists is tremendous to a company, and while I have seen companies attempt to purchase one, I have yet to ever hand one over. That's because the relationship with our editors is important. We don't want people bombarding them with the wrong pitches in an obtrusive way. Would you want someone you didn't know emailing you (or even calling) with a sales pitch for a service or product your company wouldn't use and then following up every other day, asking why you aren't answering? Probably not. That's exactly how a pitch comes across when it's a topic not relevant to the person's beat or if you follow up one too many times.

When beginning your research, start by creating a "wish list" of media outlets you foresee yourself being in. Be realistic about your goals. We have clients that come to us and say, first thing, that their top goal is to be on a national daytime talk show. They don't have a consumer-driven product, and they don't have a news hook that makes them relevant for national daytime television, so no, this is not a realistic goal for them. Your wish list should reflect the media outlets that make the most sense for your brand and that have featured similar brands before; don't add a show to your wish list simply because you are a fan. Research the reporters covering your beat, and analyze their style of writing to develop a pitch angle that falls in line with how they typically cover companies.

Professional Stalking

There are multiple ways to find key reporters. Call it "professional stalking." Start by visiting the media outlet's website and searching your industry by name. For instance, if you are in "climate" or "EdTech," then search your competitors by name to see if they've been covered by that media outlet before. This will lead you to select individuals who would be the best fit for writing about your company.

As you search your competitors' coverage, also pay attention to how the media is writing about them, as that will serve you later on as you write your pitches. Some articles will also include tags at the bottom of the article that pertain to keywords relevant to the topics of the article. When clicked on, these will show you all the past articles under that tag by that publication. While you're on the website, check for specific sections. Each media outlet is broken down a certain way, so look to see where you or your company would best fit. There are typically select individuals handling each section.

When picking the media outlets to research, don't get tunnel vision and pick only the mainstream press and the trades most relevant to you. There are also trade publications for other industries that might have a column relevant to your product or service. This opens up the number of media outlets that may cover you and increases your chances of receiving coverage. You can also go into the News section of Google and search the same key terms that you used on the media outlets' websites. This may seem like the same process, but it allows you to be more thorough in your research. It catches some articles that may not have necessarily come up on your first search. Doing this on a daily basis is also helpful, because you can monitor the daily news cycles to see who is most often covering your industry, and it may show media outlets that you didn't necessarily think of yet.

BUILDING THE RELATIONSHIP

Media people are just like us. They have feelings, they get annoyed by poor judgment, they're trying to do the best work possible, and at the end of the day, they need to get a job done. On so many occasions, I've seen publicists treat the process with a media person as if it were a transaction—as if they were going to a grocery store, picking up an item, walking to the register, paying for the item, and then walking out, likely never seeing the cashier ever again. In the PR process, the media person is an extremely important player. You need to treat them more like a family member whom you might speak with only every few months but whom you always pick right back up with, versus a one-time interaction where you are brief, less engaged, and more like strangers to one another.

Humanize the Relationship

When you initiate communication with a media person, make the cold outreach feel warm. Did you notice from LinkedIn that the reporter grew up in the same small town as you? Did you notice on Instagram that their dog just celebrated his first birthday? Did a recent article they wrote move you to take action in your personal life? Or did you notice from Instagram Stories that they are traveling next month to a place you already visited, and they are looking for recommendations? To know the answers to any of these questions means that you researched the person and their online presence to get to know them better. This tactic will allow you to start a conversation on a more personal note; your pitch shouldn't come across as one-sided and solely about you getting a media win for your client.

A media pitch is a two-way street. You have to make it a mutually beneficial relationship. If you picked up your office phone line to a sales rep calling, and the first thing you heard was a pitch about how great their product was and why you needed to buy it, you'd probably feel as though the call was a bit abrupt and would likely be taken aback. It's possible you would be annoyed, and if you didn't hang up right away, you'd likely rush that person off the call. There's no human factor in a sales call: no consideration of time, no personalized reason for why you specifically need what they are selling today, and simply no personal connection for you to rationalize giving this person two minutes that will take away time spent somewhere else.

I have an alumni organization that calls me every few months for donations. I applaud their effort to fundraise, and of course, I always donate a few dollars even if I'm in a rush, but they call at the worst times, every time. It's always after a long workday when I just got home and I'm about to sit down to relax. We're talking 8:00 p.m. calls. By that time, I've completely detached from my workday, and I want to enjoy my time doing things that pertain more to my personal life.

Receiving a call just as I sit down, from someone who called me off of their sales list, is not one of my favorite things. If the person making the calls were more strategic in their approach, they'd realize this late-night call was coming across as one-sided. Perhaps the time works for the caller's schedule, but for the person on the receiving end, it seems as if their time isn't being considered or respected. Naturally, when a first connection starts off with an off-balance sentiment like this, the call likely won't go so well.

As with all connections, humanize the interaction. In relationships, people like to feel special, so this interaction is no different. Use what you researched on the person to provide commentary and to make the outreach more about them. Get into their perspective. Based on their past articles and their social media presence, what topics do they cover, and how do they cover them? They are receiving hundreds of pitches daily, so stand out from the others.

Start by trying to make a personal connection with the person. Understand their needs and what they are looking for in the relationship. They typically want to deliver the next "big" story, or at least one that will resonate with their audiences. They are looking for content that drives clicks and traffic back to a media outlet's website. If a reporter just wrote a story about the topic you are pitching, they are likely to not cover it again anytime soon. Instead, predict their next move and their next story of interest. For instance, if you give someone a cupcake because you saw them eat cake and cookies

and know they like sweets—even if you haven't seen them eat a cupcake before—you are coming up with an assumption based on past
behaviors and habits.

Build Rapport

A media pitch should never feel like a one-sided sales call that isn't
considerate of the end receiver's time, work, and feelings. Chris
Metinko of *Crunchbase News* explains, "I think the best way to build
a rapport with a reporter is to understand what it is they are interested in reporting on and their actual needs—instead of trying to
just make something fit. Those who ask questions and truly try to
understand what someone is working on are those that are able to
build the best rapport."[1] There are a lot of unspoken rules when it
comes to rapport with the media; the following breaks down the
most important ones.

Do:

- Treat reporters like they are human beings.

- Find a common personal connection.

- Be courteous of their time.

- Take the relationship slowly and be in it for the long haul.

- Create personalized emails and content.

- Offer concise, specific details and actionable next steps.

- Offer a pitch that will help them to deliver a good story to
  their readers.

Don't:

- Treat the pitch as if it is a transaction.

- Bcc and blast out a generic pitch.

- Email someone whose beat has nothing to do with your company.

- Email out a press release and expect it to be picked up.

- Harass a reporter with outreach and follow-ups.

- Spam someone's inbox.

- Waste an editor's time with an email that doesn't make sense, has no ask, is forceful, and so on.

A common thought when sending out a pitch is, *If I send this out to as many people as possible, the odds of it being picked up will be greater.* Logically that does make sense, but realistically, it will have the opposite effect. The more people you send your pitch to, the more generic it is likely to be, and the less personalized it will sound to the reporter, who will know instantly that you did not research them. This alone will make a reporter not want to pick up the story.

What's worse than sending out a generic pitch is using the bcc line so there is no personalized "Hi, [name]" at the beginning of the email. It is also highly recommended that you don't call, email, and send a message on social media all within a short time period—for example, a ten-minute window (don't laugh, it happens)—and then do the same the next day and ask, "Did you see my email?" That's a lot, to say the least. Reporters see your email. If they like it, they'll respond. If not, take it as a "not interested."

Once you have the relationship initiated with the reporter, the next thing you need to do is maintain it. Treat it delicately during each interaction so as not to leave room for missteps that could potentially jeopardize the relationship. For instance, tapping a reporter too much to cover you will likely annoy them, and they won't want to engage with you anymore. Wait until you have a really good news item to share with them, and when you do, don't spam them with constant email replies. Be concise and organized in the emails you send back to them. Also, don't tell your friends about your new relationship. What's just as bad as you spamming them is having your friend spam them for you. Respect the relationship enough to hold it close to you.

❧❧ Innovation Station ❧❧

Part I explains that to lay the foundation for your PR strategy, you need to connect to the root of your brand's identity, humanize the connection, and consistently develop content that portrays your core messaging. Part II teaches that building your brand materials, developing your story, and analyzing your competitors sets you up for a successful execution of the PR strategy. Absolutely everything discussed in Parts I and II will go to waste if you do not know who you are speaking to and how you are speaking with them.

Relationships are part of your path to success in both your personal life and in your career. The media can play an integral part in your company's growth strategy, so it's important to research key reporters and start building the foundation for getting to know them on a more personal level. When opening a line of communication with someone, remember to keep in mind how you like to be approached and the written rapport you prefer people have with you. Reporters are the gatekeepers for you and your company to receive media coverage, so respect their boundaries and provide value to the relationship.

CHAPTER 9

The Right Pitch

Great work is unexpected.

—**PETER COUGHTER,** *The Art of the Pitch*

It's sunny when Jack walks to his first meeting of the day. He usually visits two to three medical offices daily, and this morning he woke up with confidence, feeling as though he would be selling his top offering today. Last night, Jack repeated the new sales pitch format he learned at the seminar he took over the weekend. It was a two-day workshop that focused on "winning and owning the sale." They taught a very dominating approach that guaranteed "a sale before you leave the office." Jack feels inspired and motivated from the workshop and is ready to take on the week.

When he gets to the office for his first meeting, he waits fifteen minutes past his scheduled meeting time. Then the receptionist notifies him that the person he was supposed to be meeting with is running behind in a prior meeting and will no longer be available. Jack, feeling slightly disappointed that he can't use his new pitch, brushes off the meeting and dashes across town to his next meeting.

This is going to be the one, Jack thinks to himself. He walks into the second meeting, and before he goes to sit down, the person notifies him that their company just signed a deal with another provider, so he doesn't want to waste Jack's time today.

"I completely understand," Jack tells them. "Should anything change, please let us know."

Jack finally arrives at his last meeting of the day, which, as irony would have it, is on the other side of town from where he began his day. By this point, it is the end of the day, and Jack is exhausted, but he is determined to make this meeting worthwhile. While taking the bus on his way over, Jack did a quick search online to see if the company had any recent announcements or any recent press so he could make a reference to it. He also looked up the person he was meeting with on social media. He saw the person traveled recently to see her family in Wisconsin, which Jack visited a few years back for a conference. Jack quickly looked up the names of some of the attractions he went to so it was fresh in his mind, in case he saw an opportunity to throw in a reference or two.

Jack enters the last office, and before he can sit down in the waiting room, Lucy, the woman he is scheduled to meet with, approaches him.

"Thanks for coming by today, Jack. I'm a bit ahead of schedule today, so if you don't mind, we can get started now."

"Sure thing," replies Jack.

As they walk to the meeting room, Jack says, "On my way over, I noticed on social media that you have family in Wisconsin."

Lucy is surprised and replies, "I actually do! The kids and I just came back from visiting my parents for a week. It was great seeing them. Have you been to Wisconsin?"

Jack, starting to feel as if he's onto something, says, "I went on a business trip a few years back. I had a great time and was even able to visit a few of the tourist attractions. There are some great restaurants there, too. My favorite was that one on Seventeenth Avenue."

Lucy smiles and replies, "You're kidding! I used to go there with my grandparents whenever they babysat me and my sister."

Jack and Lucy spend a few minutes reminiscing about some of the places Lucy loved as a kid growing up in Wisconsin.

Within the fifteen minutes remaining, Jack shares his main selling points for an engaging prospect, including why his innovative offering is unlike anything on the market and how it can improve efficiency as well as increase ROI. After finishing his meeting, Jack asks if he can schedule a follow-up meeting to continue the conversation. Lucy happily agrees to next week, same time.

As Jack walks out of the building that afternoon, he realizes what he learned during his weekend workshop was just part of the formula. It wasn't until after he established a personal connection with the prospect that he really saw a huge shift in their response. Yes, it will take extra time to research each person before Jack walks into each meeting, but in the end, it will be worth the higher return.

THE MEDIA PITCH

Like a sales pitch, the media pitch requires a strategy consisting of key behaviors. It will also take some outreach, because even if your pitch is perfect with all the right details, the person on the receiving end may not be paying attention or, as Jack experienced, may be stuck in a meeting and can't make time to listen to, much less read, your pitch. You have a short window of time to make a good first impression, but taking the time to build rapport with the reporter will increase the likelihood of them becoming interested in your pitch, and it will open the window for you to establish a relationship with them so you can present other pitches to them later on.

THE FIVE WS

Pitching in public relations is most frequently done via the written word, so when compiling your pitch, it needs to be concise and eye-catching. Reporters receive hundreds of pitches daily, so they can't possibly review all of them. But if they stop to review yours, you'll want to make your pitch stand out from the others. A personalized introduction letting the reporter know why you thought of them for this story, coupled with high-level details supporting your pitch and distinguishing it from any competitors, is a great way to set yourself apart from the pack. When pitching, keep the following in mind.

Who

Knowing *who* you are pitching to is as important as knowing what you are pitching. Think of the reporter's perspective as you are writing them. Do you think your pitch is personalized and shows you took the time to get to know *them* as a person and understand their writing style? Do they generally cover this topic? Does your pitch come off as one-sided without benefiting your audience? The reporter is your audience, and at the same time, the reporter's audience is your audience.

If you are pitching a story, it needs to entice the reporter *and* speak to their audience. By presenting a story that appeals to their audience, you are creating a mutually beneficial relationship. You are helping the reporter find a new story angle to give to their readers or followers. Always take into consideration just how many emails a reporter receives on any given day, because that can also affect how you write the pitch. You don't want to take too long to get to the point, and you want to be sure that your ask is clear and up front.

What

It's important to know *what* is newsworthy. The founders we work with are extremely intelligent individuals, and each one has developed a company that is truly groundbreaking. What I often see as a learning curve for them is knowing the caliber of their news and how it relates to the stage of growth their company is currently at.

For example, what is a big step for a seed-stage company may not be big enough news for a Tier-1 media outlet to cover. That doesn't mean the company will never be covered; it just means that it will take trying extra pitches and strategizing a few different story angles before the outlet will commit to writing the story.

The larger a company is, the more likely a media outlet will cover it. When writing the details of your pitch, always be sure the information you provide includes quality content with factual information, including statistics and recent studies from either your company or from a reputable organization (always crediting your source).

When

Timing can make or break a pitch, so it's important to know *when* to send a pitch and when not to. For instance, if an A-list celebrity passes away unexpectedly and the news cycles are saturated with media coverage, don't email out a pitch. It will be lost within a sea of emails that will get backed up in the reporter's inbox. Once the reporter does finish covering the celebrity's death, there are far too many emails to sort through, so unless your email looks like an existing conversation or something groundbreaking, there's a good chance it will be deleted.

For obvious reasons, natural disasters are another example of when you'd want to avoid pitching to the media. All eyes are going to be on search and rescue and whether more damage is on the way. So don't try pitching a hot story during a natural disaster, unless it pertains to the disaster.

You'll also want to consider the day of the week and the time of day. The beginning of the week is when reporters are typically look-ing for fresh stories, and by the end of the week, they're busy trying to write their stories and submit them before the close of the week. You never want to send pitches over the weekend, because they will get lost in a flood of spam. Unless it is a breaking news reporter, you can assume the person you are pitching isn't working on the weekend. The same can be said for the evenings during the week. Do you like receiving emails after work hours? Neither do reporters. Also, similar to what you may do, when reporters start their day, they look at all the emails they received overnight. Midmorning to midafternoon are safe times for sending out fresh pitch emails. You'll also want to consider the time zone of the person you are emailing and factor that into the suggested times above.

Where

Physical location doesn't matter in terms of writing an actual pitch, so for the purpose of this book, I use *where* in two different ways. First, consider where your spokespeople are in terms of their location and availability for interviews. If you are utilizing breaking news as a hook for thought leadership, then you'll need to make sure your spokespeople can quickly hop on the phone or, if they're in a major city, come into the studio for on-camera interviews.

The second "where" pertains to where you place key information in your pitch. For instance, burying the hook two paragraphs into the pitch won't grab the reader's attention in time. Reporters have many pitches to go through, so they may not read your entire email. Therefore, it's imperative that the most important information be highlighted at the start of the pitch. You will grab the reader's attention, and that alone will convince them to keep reading.

Why

When drafting an email pitch, your "why" should be considered throughout. You should state *why* you are emailing the reporter within the first few sentences of your pitch. In the body of the pitch, include details on why your story is important enough to be written about, which should be conveyed by the uniqueness of your offering.

Insider Tips and Tricks

I had the opportunity to speak with Scott Omelianuk, editor-in-chief of *Inc.* magazine, who is also a consultant for startup companies and a startup lecturer at universities like the Stevens Institute of Technology. When I spoke with Scott about the pitches he receives that stand out, he said, "They have a level of personalization, and they display a greater awareness of what the brand is doing. The pitches aren't created in a way that suggests a transactional exchange."[1]

He says he deletes most of the pitches he receives without even reading past the subject line. He often receives emails asking, "Are you working on any stories about entrepreneurs?" If you've read *Inc.* magazine, then you know their content targets entrepreneurs. It's safe to assume their editorial team is always working on stories about entrepreneurs, so a question like this is too general to warrant a response back and is actually a gross oversight on the part of the person sending the pitch.

The most successful relationships Scott has with communications people never start with a pitch about a particular client. Aside from adding the personal element, the pitch reads as if the person is offering help and support that would be useful to Scott and his team. That tone automatically takes away a bristling reaction he normally has when he does read pitches, because nothing is being asked of him at that given moment.

Editors-in-chief have dozens of people asking them things constantly, so when communications people position themselves as a helpful resource rather than another ask, Scott is more likely to have a rapport with them. When someone takes the time, makes themselves a resource, and allows Scott the time to learn about who they represent and why, he can later direct an editor from his team back to that person when he sees an opportunity for there to be a fit in a story.

When Scott first started in his role as editor-in-chief, he had a publicist reach out to him to ask for ten to fifteen minutes of his time. During that time, she introduced herself, asked him what direction he was taking the brand in, and what that meant in terms of the kind of stories they would write. During her interview, she only tangentially spoke about her clients. Scott felt this was useful because he got to know her and could sense how much trust he could place in her. He could also tell that she wasn't just trying to get an immediate media hit out of him or, worse, make her next "transaction." This particular relationship developed over time, and eventually Scott would turn to her for a question or two of his own when it came to getting advice on speaking engagements, since he knew that was in her wheelhouse.

It's this kind of mutually respectful relationship that allows Scott to feel comfortable having an open dialogue with someone about their client or pitch. He's able to say no to them, and if they push back, he'll give them the opportunity to change his mind. As he explains, "The fact is, we know our audience better than you do. We have no interest in making founders look bad, so we try to find the right fits, but it's a non-transactional process that takes place over time."

My conversation with Scott evolved from the importance of relationship-building and rapport to the very popular question he gets from startup companies: "What is the ROI on PR?"

Scott said, "The right metric is rarely just about raw impressions. It's that, combined with the right audience and the right kind of coverage. Coverage that enhances credibility and coverage that explains their company message in a way that encourages people to further engage with the company off of the media platform."

Scott reminds us that a media opportunity is not just a "plug and play," stating, "It doesn't matter how many people see it. It is about it being the right people. It takes someone who has the savvy to understand the real ROI on media relations, the real business opportunities that come from it, and the real human interaction that is required to tell the story."

THE PRESS RELEASE

When startup companies begin working with us, they consistently say, "Let's put out a press release." Little do they realize that a press release does not produce the same results as it used to. It's an old-school PR tactic that is still being used by some professionals simply because that's what they've always done.

Traditionally, when a press release was issued, it would go out on the wire service or be sent out to the news desks and then to reporters. That's how writers became aware of news announcements. They would, in turn, choose to write about the story based on the press release and the content provided. These days, the world is cluttered with information, and because there are so many pitch emails being sent to reporters and announcements being issued, a press release no longer holds the same weight it once did.

There are only two instances when I suggest a press release be written for our clients: (1) if their investors want to see it up on a media outlet source, they couldn't get the story picked up through pitching the editorial team, and they want to increase SEO, or (2) if it is used as supplementary material for a PR pitch or investor materials.

Before deciding on what to do with your press release, you will first want to determine if your announcement is newsworthy. If you are a venture-backed company and are announcing a new round of funding, then a press release is an absolute necessity. Media outlets want the press release as something to review for consideration, because it is fact based and has all the statistics in relation to the announcement. Pre-seed and seed rounds are harder to secure media coverage for within the Tier-1 media, but not impossible. If the company has a unique offering that will solve a problem for a large demographic, you can leverage the innovation as part of your story angle. As you can imagine, the more money involved in the funding and the higher the round being raised, the easier it becomes for the story to be picked up by a major media outlet.

With many of our clients, we see releases related to the appointment of new executives to the C-suite, which is huge for the company but not necessarily for the media. Unless you are a Fortune 500 company, the media likely will not cover news of your newly appointed vice president of marketing. In this case, if investors want the announcement made and for it to live somewhere online, then a press release to a wire service would make sense. However, if you are a local retailer hosting an event at your establishment, then a press release is not necessary; you can email the media with personal invites, and you won't need a national wire service for something that is happening locally.

Wire Services

If you give a customized pitch to reporters about the announcement but don't receive any interest, then a press release on the wire is beneficial for making sure the announcement lives somewhere online other than on your own website or social media channels. The most widely used wire services are PR Newswire and Business Wire. The price of a press release over a reputable wire service can come with a hefty price tag, but it will help increase SEO for the key search terms relative to the announcement. That press release will also be distributed to numerous credible media outlets, or as we say, "The release will be picked up."

The only stipulation with this is that the release will live on the back end of the media outlets, and it won't come up on the homepage of the media outlet. It will, however, show up when searched for. Because of the cost, I don't suggest this route for companies with a limited budget. There are free wire services that, when posted to, will allow what is posted to come up in a Google search, but it will not be picked up by any other media outlets. At the time of this writing, such wire services include PR.com and PRLog.com. Wire services that have a substantially lower fee are PRUnderground.com and EINPressWire.com.

Formatting

Reporters prefer to receive customized pitches and not just a copy and paste of a press release into the body of an email. This is why if a press release is created about the announcement, it's better to attach the file to the actual pitch email. If a reporter wants to pull a pre-approved quote or factual information/statistics to include within their story, they can refer back to the press release.

When writing a press release, start by including your logo at the top left and the press contact on the top right. If you are the founder of the company, never use your personal information. Instead use that of a team member, or if you are a team of one, then the general office email and phone line. The logo and the press contact should be on the same lines. Under the logo, include "NOT FOR IMMEDIATE RELEASE" while you are drafting the document. Once the release is finalized, then you can take out the "not."

The information included within the press releases will be formatted based around the news and materials you have available for inclusion, but in general, the title of the release is in bold and a larger-size font, while the subtitle is standard and italicized. The title briefly mentions the company name and what the announcement is; the subtitle provides slightly more detail. The body of the release starts with the city and state and then the date the announcement is being made in written form, including month, day, and year. The first line of the press release reads differently from the title and subtitle, providing more substance and including a hyperlink to the company website and the company's one-liner. The first paragraph is three to five sentences and includes to-the-point information on the who, what, where, when, and why. The second paragraph includes specific details elaborating on what was already shared in paragraph one. A quote is then included from the founder or another C-suite executive, explaining why this announcement is important and what this will mean for the future.

The next paragraph can contain details about your company's history, referencing any big awards or achievements accomplished to date. If there are any other companies included in the announcement, you can include a quote from their spokesperson, or if you want, you can include a short quote from a top customer. A closing statement to the release indicates where people can find more information on you—that is, whether they can visit your website or email a general inbox or someone directly. The company's boilerplate "About" info will be the final content added. To mark the close of the release, type "##" in the center of the line to designate its finale.

Sample Press Release

[Logo here]

Press Contact:
[Name of contact]
[Company name]
[Email address]
[Phone number]

FOR IMMEDIATE RELEASE

TITLE

Subtitle

City, State (Date of announcement)—[Company name, hyperlinked back to the website], [one-liner about the company] announced today _____.

[Supporting information]

"[Insert first sentence of quotation]," said [Name], founder and CEO of [Company name]. "[Continue quotation]."

[Company history and accolades]

[Additional quotations]

For additional information, please visit www.yourwebsite.com or email name@yourcompany.com.

About:
[Insert company boilerplate]

##

Pitching the Exclusive

When using the press release as a supplemental pitch tactic, there are three ways you can position your email to reporters. You can put that day's date on the press release and just start sending it out to everyone. While ambitious, this isn't very strategic, and if we've learned anything during our time together, it's that PR is strategic.

The second option is to pitch the story as an *embargoed exclusive*. This means you are giving the rights to a reporter to write a story and release it before anyone else has had the opportunity to do so. It is more of a "handshake" deal and is a mutually respected agreement between both parties: the media person and the person offering them the story, usually the publicist or, in this case, you. Some media outlets do not require the "exclusive" for them to cover it, but typically the more top-tier (also known as Tier-1) the media outlet is, the more likely they are to require it.

The embargoed exclusive is offered to one person at a time. It becomes quite the dilemma when you have competing media outlets interested in an exclusive, and you have to decline one, explaining that you chose their competitor over them. You can guarantee you'll never work with that media outlet again. When deciding who to pitch the exclusive to, start with your wish list of media outlets, and list them out in order of priority.

Send the first pitch to the top person on your list. Within that email, mention that you're offering them an embargoed exclusive, and also mention it within your main subject line: Embargoed Exclusive: [Company name and announcement]. Additionally, within the press release that you attach to the pitch, change the text where you originally put "NOT FOR IMMEDIATE RELEASE" to "EMBARGOED

EXCLUSIVE." Allow one to two days for your first media person to receive and review your pitch before sending a follow-up email. If you do not hear back from that person after two follow-ups, then try another person at the media outlet. All individuals you reach out to should be targeted individuals who cover your type of news announcement. Once you've contacted all possible prospects from that one media outlet, then go to the next media outlet on your wish list. Continue as such before evaluating your next possible steps.

Once you secure an exclusive with a media outlet, the reporter will ask when you need the story released by. You can tell them the formal date of the announcement, or you can allow for flexibility and let them know you can work around their scheduling, since some media outlets may pass simply because they can't turn around an article in time for the date you want it released.

It's important to remember that you need the story more than the reporter does, so you can't expect them to do what you say as if they were your hired employee. They don't work for you, so naturally, they don't have to do anything you say. Treat them like human beings, and be understanding of the fact that they have large workloads that they need to get through. If they like your pitch enough, they will stop to add it into the mix.

I wouldn't suggest jeopardizing a lead just because of a date you insist on happening. No one likes forceful individuals, so if possible, be flexible with the reporter. After the story is out, all media outlets are free to write their stories. This means you can then change the press release attachment to "FOR IMMEDIATE RELEASE" with the formal date the announcement was made and remove all references to "exclusives" within your email pitches.

The third option for pitching an announcement is contacting all media outlets with the press release under "Embargo until [date]." The difference here is that you are giving an opportunity to all media outlets to cover the announcement at the same time. The caveat is that the media outlets that require exclusives may not cover it, but the bonus is that should the announcement not be big enough for a Tier-1 publication to cover as an embargoed exclusive, you still have the opportunity to obtain coverage from several smaller media outlets on the day you want the announcement made. Similar to the embargoed exclusive, you would label all documents and pitches with the embargo date. Interviews can be done in advance, and you can let the reporter know their stories shouldn't run until after your embargo date.

❢❢ Innovation Station ❡❡

When sending a pitch to a reporter, look at it as being the only shot you have with that person. This way, you treat the pitch delicately and are more intentional with what you put into it. It's always important to provide accurate and specific information at all times. If you are waiting to receive a confirmation on a small detail, always wait to receive that information *before* sending it to a reporter.

Your pitch should be thorough but to the point and include the five *W*s. Along with emailing specific pitch stories to reporters, you can also use third-party platforms where reporters post inquiries on companies or experts they are looking to include within the story they are already working on. Such websites include HARO (Help a

Reporter Out), ProfNet, and Qwoted. You can also pitch on Twitter by following the hashtag #JournoRequests and responding via DM to the media person's request. It's similar in theory to how you would email a reporter, except you're using sound bites instead of long pitches, and your inbox is your direct messages.

{ Part IV }

DELIVER

CHAPTER 10

Follow Through

Not following up . . . is the same as filling up your
bathtub without first putting the stopper in the drain.

—MICHELLE MOORE, *Selling Simplified*

After a long day of work, Joanna looks down at her watch and
realizes it's nearly seven o'clock, two hours after everyone else
in her office has clocked out. Joanna really wants a promotion and is
hoping that her bosses notice how hard she is working in her current
position. She is exhausted from the extra hours she's been putting in,
but Joanna will do whatever it takes to impress her bosses.

The problem with this scenario is that no one knows Joanna wants
a promotion, because she never *told* anyone. Her bosses think she is
doing an amazing job, and if there's anything that needs to be completed in a timely fashion, they know they can rely on Joanna for just
that. She's become their go-to person for those in-a-pinch situations.

Unfortunately, Joanna's bosses see her as solely that: a pinch hitter. In fact, they haven't envisioned anything else for her, because they think Joanna loves what she does, since she does it so well.

Ava, on the other hand, is Joanna's colleague who holds a very similar position, but she usually leaves each day around five thirty. Ava also seems to work really hard but doesn't put in as many extra hours as Joanna does. In Joanna's mind, she far exceeds Ava in the role. What Joanna doesn't know is the personal conversations Ava has had with her bosses behind closed doors. Since joining the company a year ago, Ava has expressed to her superiors her interest in a more senior-level position. Ava continuously has regular meetings with her boss, who has become a bit of a mentor to her, and they review her progress together. Because Ava made her goals known, she is being primed for a promotion should a position become available, whereas Joanna is being overlooked because she never expressed an interest in anything other than her current job.

We can all relate to Joanna, because she really wants a promotion, even though it requires extra work and usually more hours. The disconnect for her happened, however, when she failed to tell her superiors her goals. While her bosses do their best to create an inclusive and supportive environment, they have their own day-to-day roles to manage, so unless Joanna takes a moment to tell them how she's feeling, they'll continue to go about their day, oblivious to her professional goals. Because Ava presented her goals, followed up, and did the work to see it through, she eventually earned the promotion that she laid the foundation for.

Some of you may be wondering what this has to do with PR. Well, pretty much everything. The PR version of Joanna is the person who has a great story to tell but no audience to share it with and doesn't know how to get media coverage around it. Ava is the skilled individual who can make any story pressworthy by talking to as many people as possible, and she puts in the work until it happens. In PR, you want to be an Ava. It's a long-term process to go from sending your first media pitch to securing a feature story. It's in between those two touchpoints where strategy, craft, and skill come into play.

FOLLOW-UP STAGES

The follow-up process is the longest stage of the PR cycle. As we've learned from prior chapters, the PR cycle starts by building press materials during the ramp-up phase. Next, you will need to do some research to find the proper media contacts to pitch to. And after you hit Send on your first email to a reporter, you automatically enter what is called the *follow-up* stage.

Truthfully, this is the most frustrating part of the process and one that can really separate the good publicists from the bad. This is where emotions start to show; you'll see desperation in those pleading with a reporter to cover their story, and aggressiveness in those who are virtually stalking a reporter. You're eager to secure a media hit, and that's understandable, but if your eagerness overpowers the pitch, it will do more harm than good.

You can't put a set amount of time on how long the follow-up stage will take, because every pitch is different. One thing I can tell you, though, is that it takes a whole lot of patience and consistency over a long period of time. There are pitches I've worked on for over eight months, and even then I didn't receive 100 percent confirmation until the issue hit newsstands. Knowing how to follow up is key for a number of reasons. Here are just a few of them:

- A reporter may not see a pitch unless you flag it for them, again.

- If you follow up too many times in too short of a time span, the behavior will appear aggressive and turn off a reporter.

- If you don't answer an interview request in time, the reporter may find someone else who is available sooner.

- If you aren't following up with new and relevant news angles, then you are wasting time on a stale pitch that a reporter is ignoring.

Fear of Rejection

When I meet novice publicists, one of the biggest hurdles they have to being successful in their work is getting over the judgment that comes along with the job. Like a salesperson, a publicist or anyone who is pitching to the media will receive more noes than yeses. Some of the emotions often experienced include feeling *ignored* from not having a pitch answered, *anxious* over the possibility of annoying a reporter, *fear* of not getting a media placement at all, *discouraged* from receiving a pass, and many others. It's hard not to take the pitching process personally. As human beings, we deal with the emotions that come from rejection in our personal lives all the time, and in PR, that feeling is no different. Similar to life, in PR you learn to develop a thick skin from years of being told no and from a few rude, potentially nasty comments in between.

Rejection is inevitable in the pitching process. Even when you think you have the best news hook and you've found the perfect reporter to pitch it to, it doesn't always work out as you initially planned. Sometimes that perfectly suited reporter may not even respond to you. It's not personal, and there can be a number of reasons for their not responding to you. Reporters can receive upward of a hundred pitches per day, so it may come down to something as simple as having missed your email. Some reporters may even delete a handful of emails at a time without even reading them, just to clean out their inbox. Think about when you go into the inbox of the personal email address you use to sign up for sales and promotions. You probably receive dozens of emails in just one day that you may not even read the subject line of before deleting. How you feel going through that inbox is the same way a reporter feels going through their inbox!

This is a prime example of why you need to send a follow-up email. A reporter does not delete all their emails, but there's a chance they may have done so to your initial query. If the email does get reviewed, then there is the potential for the reporter to provide you with feedback. Not all reporters will respond with a formal decline. Sometimes no response simply implies a "no." You won't know this, though, unless you go through the follow-up process. Then, after several attempts, you can safely assume they aren't interested. And that's okay. Simply move on to the next reporter.

Remember: You can't control everything in the PR process, and you certainly can't make a reporter respond to you. You can put in the best effort possible to nudge them, but at the end of the day, they are in charge of their inbox. Sending an email is their decision to make.

PR can feel a bit like an emotional roller coaster at times, and I say that in the best way possible. There's no better feeling than landing a large media placement with a top-tier media outlet, but it takes time to get to that moment. I often tell newer publicists after they've received their first media pitch decline, "Brush it off. Don't think about it, and just move on to the next." I say this because you can't waste time dwelling on those moments or, worse, allowing the fear of rejection to prevent you from properly managing the PR media-placement cycle.

Insider Tips and Tricks

Anna Medaris Miller is a coach at the New York Writing Room and a national reporter from media news websites such as U.S. News, Insider, and Women's Health. She also has appeared on the *Today Show* and *Good Morning America*. These days, as a senior health reporter at Insider, Anna describes a typical day as "writing one to two stories, doing follow-up on past stories and outreach for future ones, conducting interviews and attending meetings, and reacting to any breaking news relevant to my beat."[1]

Reading, let alone thoughtfully reviewing, pitch emails—which come in at a rate of about one a minute—is rarely a top priority. Most, she admits, she deletes without even opening. For the pitches she likes to receive, she wants the ask to be clear and up front: "Tell me what you're actually pitching. Are you pitching yourself as an expert, or are you pitching a feature on a product and/or business?"

Also, be sure to use plain language and proofread your work! You'd be surprised at how often someone has called her the wrong name! Some of the not-so-obvious dos and don'ts of pitching include "thinking outside of the email." She'll often post what she's looking for on Twitter, get ideas through Instagram, and make connections through real-life events. Also, she says, "Be open to wildly different angles. The story that runs may evolve into something different than originally planned."

One major thing Anna expressed was first emphasized by a fellow reporter, *The New York Times*' Taylor Lorenz, who said, "Your success is not a story."

"These are not stories, they're PR," Lorenz wrote in her Substack newsletter. "Unless your story ties into some larger cultural trend, or holds some type of important wider significance, I am not interested in covering it. And frankly, it's not newsworthy."[2] Take a step back, and think about why a reader cares about your story, rather than why you want your story to be told.

After the First Pitch

You did your research, crafted the perfect pitch, and officially sent out your first media pitch. Now what? You may feel a huge rush of energy and excitement come over you as you anticipate the responses that will come pouring in. One hour goes by, then two, and before you know it, it's the end of the day, and you haven't heard back from anyone. You can't help but feel slightly disappointed, and that's completely normal. Reporters need time to sort through the emails in their inbox, let alone manage the assignments they are given. They also must schedule and take interviews for the stories they already have in place, and they need to actually have their story written in time to submit before their deadline. All of that has to be managed in a single day, so while you may be sitting at your computer eagerly awaiting a response, keep in mind, the person on the other end likely isn't sitting there waiting for your email.

Now that you've sent your first email to a reporter, you have to figure out a way to get their attention to ensure they both see the pitch and spend a moment reading it. The best first step is to courteously give the reporter the time to both see and read the email themselves. After two or three days, it's safe to send a follow-up email. If the reporter doesn't answer, it doesn't mean they are not interested. It can take a number of rounds of follow-ups before the person answers. You want to space the follow-up emails out adequately enough so you don't come across as aggressive. As time goes on, add more days in between the follow-ups. For example, your second follow-up can be three to five days from your first.

After a few attempts, though, you do have to consider that perhaps the person just isn't interested. You may want to give it a break and work on revamping your pitch or creating a new story angle. Then you can revisit the idea of pitching the person at a later time. It can take a few different approaches to secure a placement. The more you attempt to get to know the reporter, whether by email or over social media, and the more outreach attempts you make (over the long term, not in a short time frame) with adequate story angles, the more likely a story will come to fruition. It's basically a numbers game. The more you put out there, the more likely you'll receive something in return.

How Many?

If one reporter from a media outlet declines or simply doesn't answer, that doesn't always mean it's a closed door on the media outlet as a whole. For national media outlets, there are dozens or, in some cases, hundreds of people who work there. So, when one person says no, it's okay to try someone else. What you don't want to do is pitch everyone all at once. If you do that, you risk coming across as too aggressive.

By now you've probably noticed a theme. Let me reiterate: *Don't do anything that could potentially annoy a reporter!*

There are a number of ways a reporter can find out you pitched to someone else. Reporters sometimes forward pitch emails to their colleagues who they think might like the pitch. If the other person sees that they were already sent the pitch, then you may have to explain why you sent it to so many people at once. The reporter may also feel as though you didn't research them well enough, since it looks as if you sent the pitch to everyone you could find. When you do this, you aren't using a humanized approach. In turn, the reporter doesn't feel a personal connection to you.

So, think of the person on the receiving end when you send out your pitches. When you send it to the first person, you can even let them know they are the "first to receive" the story. Not only are you making them feel good by choosing them as your first pick, but also you are confirming that the story hasn't appeared anywhere else. Reporters prefer to be the first to cover a story, not second and definitely not third. Therefore, prioritize your asks and proceed accordingly.

Know the Tone

I'm sure you have one or two stories you could share about an unpleasant experience with a salesperson. Maybe one even sounds like this: You walk into the store and are greeted instantly by the person standing by the front door. You say hello back, and because you're on a mission to find a new pair of jeans, you go straight to that department. You initially thought it would be an easy transaction, but when you find the cut of jeans you want and your size isn't there, you need a salesperson's help to find out if there are any others in the back room. When you look up and don't see a salesperson, you go back to the front door, since you can guarantee the greeter will still be there.

You let them know your size isn't there and politely ask for their help in looking for it elsewhere. The salesperson tells you that while they can't leave the front of the store, they'll ask another associate to look in the back. In the meantime, you make yourself busy looking through some of the other clothing items nearby. You get so distracted by this that you forget how long you've been waiting. You look at your watch and realize you walked into the store roughly fifteen minutes ago; you can't imagine it would take that long to look in the back. You look up, gaze around, and notice the salesperson that offered to help you is now talking to another salesperson. You walk over and politely ask if they found your size. They respond, "One second," while putting their finger up to reinforce the statement.

Naturally, you are taken aback. You may even think to yourself, *That tone was a tad harsh considering how polite I was being.* If the salesperson had taken another approach and explained that they, along with the other salesperson, were discussing where the jeans could be found in the back room, since they were having some difficulty finding them, you likely wouldn't have thought twice about the store's customer service. But now, based on the tone of *one* person, you're questioning the *entire* store. Your experience has become less than what you anticipated, and you're not looking forward to coming back.

The moral of the story is that your tone can completely change the quality of an interaction that someone has with you. While you may not realize in the moment how your tone will be perceived by the other person, it's important to think about it before hitting Send on any email or issuing any type of communication. If there's potential for ambiguity, then assume the message will be delivered wrong. Whatever the message is that you decide to send, make sure the intentions are clear.

In terms of your PR follow-up emails, it is better to err on the side of caution and be both professional and polite in your communication. In addition, you can remind the reporter that you are available to assist with answering any questions or providing them with any information to help make for a smooth process. You can also be respectful of their time by keeping your emails concise, organized, and to the point.

Reporters also like when you are giving them content that hasn't been featured anywhere else, so remind them if it's exclusive and include a new element of information to help add more content for the writer to pull from. The more there is, the more they can envision how the story can be rounded out in a unique way. A reporter doesn't want to write the same story as someone else. They want their story to be new, fresh, and different, so share how that can be.

Example

Your email will change depending on who you are talking to and the information you are presenting. However, a general follow-up email is much shorter in length than your initial pitch. You can use the same email thread so that your original pitch is at the bottom of the email. Your follow-up email will summarize your pitch, include a new bit of information, and offer your assistance. Communication is best when customized, so here is one example of what a follow-up email can look like. However, please note: It is a template.

> Hi, [Reporter],
>
> I am following up on my email regarding [Company name] and a story on [brief explanation]. With the formal announcement taking place in just two weeks, I would like to offer you the exclusive on covering it for [Name the news outlet].
>
> Aside from the information I included below, I would like to offer you the latest report issued by [Name of your company] that indicates [something big]. Our CEO, [Name], is available for phone or email interviews to discuss the details. No other media outlet has yet received this report.
>
> Thank you again, and I appreciate the time you took to review the content of this pitch. Please let me know if I can assist you with any questions or the coordination of an interview.
>
> Best,
> [Your name]

General Rules When Following Up with Reporters

Here are some general rules for following up on media pitches:

- *Don't take things personally.* Like all business, you can't take the PR process personally. As long as you dot all your i's and cross all your t's, you know it's not your fault should there be a breakdown in the pitching process, or the media placement doesn't come to fruition. Instead of fretting about a missed opportunity, learn from the process and move on to the next pitch.

- *Have patience.* It's very easy to get frustrated or anxious when pitching. If you notice that happening, take a step back, trust the process, and stay consistent with the outreach and follow-up processes. Allow enough time between each touchpoint you have with a single reporter to give them the opportunity to review and digest the information.

- *Build rapport.* No one likes being contacted by someone who comes off as pushy, so don't be that person. Be polite in your words and patient in the process. Make the process enjoyable for everyone involved.

- *Make your pitch clear and detailed.* Be thorough in the information you provide to a reporter. Keep it organized and easy to read. Don't make it feel overwhelming or hard to digest. The easier you make it for the reporter, the more likely they will want to work with you time and time again. This is one way to build a long-term relationship with a journalist.

- *Be prepared.* Don't tell a reporter someone is available for an interview and then be difficult in scheduling it or, worse, not deliver on the person you originally promised. Be ready to respond and deliver in a timely fashion from the time a reporter responds.

❧❧ Innovation Station ☙☙

A media pitch can really make or break your chances during the follow-up stages. If you let too much time pass from the time you send your first email to when you send your second, you risk becoming old news and being completely forgotten. If you follow up too soon, you risk being a bother to the person on the receiving end. PR is a delicate balance of managing relationships while also managing the media-placement process. Since each media person operates differently, there is no set template or process to follow. However, there are best practices and things you should avoid doing to help set you up for successful media relations.

The number-one rule is to humanize your interactions. By doing so, you'll be able to put yourself in the other person's shoes, which will help you better understand how to manage your communications during the pitching process.

CHAPTER 11

Make an Impression

It takes twenty years to build a reputation
and five minutes to ruin it.

—WARREN BUFFETT, to his son Howie

Entering the interior decorator's store, I was interested in finding out about wallpaper, since my first-floor bathroom needed some sprucing up. I was initially leaning toward a bright paint, but because I was hearing so much about wallpaper in the magazines I read, I thought I would look into it as a second option. Who knows? Maybe a print would stand out to me as I was looking. After the owner walked over to introduce herself, I began explaining I was just looking. I was curious about the prints she offered and, overall, what the pricing and process looked like, since I'd never had wallpaper installed in my house before.

She showed me some options and gave me some samples to take home to see how they would look in the bathroom. There were a few I thought could work, and the pricing wasn't bad, but I wanted to see how the bathroom would look with the sample on the actual wall. I thanked the woman on the way out and told her I would be in touch if I decided to move forward. I walked out, got in my car, started driving, and five minutes later received a phone call through my car's Bluetooth. I answered, not knowing the number, and a gentleman introduced himself as someone who installs wallpaper; he asked when I wanted to schedule a time for him to come to my house to give me an estimate on installation.

I have to admit, I was a little taken aback. I give the man credit for being proactive toward a sale, but where the interior decorator went wrong was that she assumed I would be buying wallpaper from her. What appears to have happened was that as soon as I left her store, she called the wallpaper installer and passed along my phone number. I never approved her doing such, and she definitely didn't mention someone would be calling me.

The interior decorator had a lead with me as a potential buyer, but instead of strategically owning the relationship with me directly, she passed me along. This ended up annoying me, causing her approach to backfire. Long story short, I did not end up going back, and the owner lost a sale, because the process wasn't handled properly. I didn't feel as if it was a personal experience (the human factor) but rather a transaction.

The same can be said for public relations. Don't assume the media placement is a done deal just because someone showed interest. Until the media placement runs, anything can happen, and there will always be a chance that your story may not run. For this reason, you must treat the entire process delicately and as a high priority.

YOU'VE GOT THE LEAD: NOW WHAT?

A reporter responds to your pitch, but before you jump out of your chair with excitement, you should take a moment to assess what the reporter has to say. A home run would be if the response read something like "This sounds great. Can we schedule an interview?" That naturally makes for a quicker process, but it won't always be that easy. Sometimes, there are a few transitional emails back and forth with the reporter. For instance, the reporter may have some clarifying questions, and other times they may say, "I'm on deadline and will get back to you next week." If this is the case, allow them the time to get back to you, and buffer in an extra day or two to account for anything they were working on that may have been delayed. If a good amount of time goes by and you still haven't heard from the reporter, then it's safe to casually check back in with a follow-up email. If a reporter responds and tells you this isn't something they would cover, consider asking them what they do like to cover so you know how to best pitch them moving forward.

You may also hear a reporter say something along the lines of "This sounds interesting. I'll keep this on file for future." That's always a perplexing one to hear, because you would think if the person was, in fact, interested in the story, they would want to write about it. And what does "filing it away" actually mean?

Well, to answer the latter, reporters are inundated with stories they were assigned prior to your email, so it could be a matter of timing. They just aren't able to get to it. Another reason could be that while there's an aspect of the story the reporter likes, it may not be baked enough to warrant coverage. Another reporter may feel differently, however.

In terms of "filing it," that phrase means exactly what it sounds like. They're saving the email for their records. They aren't deleting it, which says a lot; they receive hundreds of emails a day, so your email certainly stood out. When this happens, the next thing to figure out is how to stay top of mind for the reporter so they don't forget your pitch when it's weeks or months later. Tactics you can take to do so include the following:

- Sending updates on new company news or announcements

- Utilizing breaking news to make the story time sensitive

- Sharing a new press hit, so long as it's not a media outlet that competes with them

- Finding new stats or additional items to round out the story with

Just as in the sales process, one wrong move leading up to the closing of the deal and you risk losing it all. A media placement is not a done deal until the moment it actually runs. There's always the chance of a story not happening. This could be due to the reporter changing their mind, your story changing, or uncontrollable factors, such as a reporter being reassigned to a different story. One reason a reporter may decide not to run a story, even if they initially expressed interest, is that perhaps they couldn't find enough information to write a full story that would be interesting enough to readers. This can be prevented on your end by ensuring there is enough material or interview content to offer the reporter at the onset of the relationship.

Another reason a story may not see the light of day is because of breaking news. Sometimes, world-changing events take place on the day your story is set to go live. I know, what are the odds? The risk is low, but for publicists who have been doing this sort of thing for years and have hundreds of stories under their belt, this has likely happened to them a handful of times. When breaking news happens, there is a chance the normal coverage is put on hold and sometimes never rescheduled.

For example, I had a doctor I was working with back in 2013 who was geared up for her first national morning show appearance. Very rarely does breaking news interrupt the national morning shows, but that day there was a pivotal moment in the Ebola outbreak. The client was so excited to finally see all her hard work come to fruition. She had done regional television and most recently national business networks, but a national morning show on daytime television was her number-one goal when she first started doing PR. We were on set. She was hair-and-makeup ready, and she absolutely nailed the interview.

Moments later, we went to check our phones, only to realize that people in New York didn't see the segment. The breaking news announcement interrupted the regularly scheduled program in a handful of markets, including New York. While the segment did not air where she lived in New York and her family and friends did not get to watch it, the segment still aired in select markets across the country. Plus, the segment went up online afterward. While this was a frustrating moment from the PR side, there were still positive takeaways from it: The doctor now had her foot in the door with the producers, who saw she was a reliable and great-on-camera expert. Because of this, the doctor got called back a few weeks later.

Whatever can be controlled from your end, I advise doing so. For instance, being easy to work with and easily accessible are two things you can do to ensure a more seamless process. You'd be surprised at how many people pitch reporters and then don't promptly respond when a reporter expresses interest. If your response is too delayed, you run the risk of a reporter losing interest or, worse, finding your competitor as a replacement. When a reporter asks for something "promptly," it means they need it as soon as possible. Reporters understand you may not be sitting at your desk watching your inbox for their reply, but they do realize most people have email on their phones. So, while you may not be able to respond to the reporter within the first five minutes, within a minimal number of hours is optimal for making a good impression.

Also, should a reporter need to schedule an interview, make your availability based on their schedule. One way to know if you are being too difficult when it comes to scheduling is to look at the number of back-and-forth emails about it. A good rule of thumb is to keep emails to a minimum.

INTERVIEW FORMATS

When a reporter confirms a story, they will either pull information directly from the press materials or ask to coordinate times for an interview with a company spokesperson. That interview can be done a number of different ways depending on the category of media: television, print, or radio/podcast.

In-Person Interview

If a reporter is local, they may want to meet you in person so they can have a more personalized interaction with you. If you have a brick-and-mortar store, it may even be a good idea for the spokesperson to be interviewed there. This way, when the reporter goes back to write their story, they can include nuances they witnessed about your business while there. It's common for reporters of local newspapers or magazines to meet in person. They'll either take notes the old-fashioned way with paper and pen or ask to audio-record the conversation. Some reporters may ask to bring a photographer or simply take photos with their phone to use alongside their written article.

Phone or Virtual Interview

Some reporters may not live close by, especially if it's a national media outlet that may be out of state. In this case, in person is not feasible, and a phone or video call is the next best thing. For those who are local and can't meet in person, it's usually because they are on a tight deadline and don't have the bandwidth to accommodate the travel time needed for an in-person meeting. While phone and virtual interviews are popular for print and online publications because of their ease, they've become a standard format for radio interviews and now for podcasts.

Written Interview

When a reporter is looking for quick responses, they will email you a list of questions to answer, along with a deadline to get it back to them by. You'll see this often for print and online reporters, and typically it's for inclusion within a much larger story. This can look like a general trend piece about the industry, and you are providing a quote as commentary on the topic. Because the story isn't entirely about you, the reporter doesn't need to do much research on you or spend time conducting a formal in-person or phone interview. A written statement suits their needs perfectly, as it helps them round out their story by including short quotes from outside sources with varying perspectives.

Video Interview

Interviews done with a video camera can be live or prerecorded. When it's prerecorded, you have the luxury of stopping to think about the questions or redoing your response if you mess up. There's less pressure with this type of interview, as opposed to when it's live and you only have one chance to get it right. TV interviews can be done either in studio or out in the field. When the cameras are sent to you or arranged at a different location from the studio, that is when you can redo takes, because that footage will be edited and packaged. A packaged segment is the final ready-to-air segment that is clean of errors and of that dead air space that happens when people think or transition between topics.

For local television networks, when someone is going in studio, it is for a lifestyle morning or afternoon talk show. Guests may be asked to sit down on a couch for what is called a *sit-down* interview, or they may be there to present a *tabletop* segment. Exactly how it sounds, a tabletop segment involves a table displaying items or products. The guest walks the host from one end of the table to the other and talks about each item. How many items are on the table depends on how long the segment is and how quickly the guest and host walk through each. Depending on the station, there may or may not be an audience.

With national television stations, there is the traditional talk show that has both the sit-down interview and tabletop segment formats, as well as the one-on-one interview. If you were to turn on a national business news network, you'd likely see a host sitting behind a desk interviewing an expert who was brought on to discuss a specific topic. Depending on the angles of the camera and how far apart they are sitting, you may see both the host and the expert together on-screen. For a closer view, the producers may zoom in on each person and show just them speaking, or they may even do a split screen.

Thanks to the vast world of the Internet, television interviews can now be done virtually. Traditionally, experts needed to be in the actual studio, typically located in a major city, and it was often common for people to fly in last minute just to make the media opportunity. A big fear of some guests was having to say no and then losing any future chance of being on the program. As you can imagine, that is not as much of a worry these days. Many networks are now accustomed to virtual interviews and have incorporated a hybrid model of both in-person and virtual interviews. Some podcasts may even have a video recording, so it can air on some platforms as just an audio interview and on others with the visual component.

INTERVIEW TIPS: VERBAL AND NONVERBAL COMMUNICATION

As we've learned, reporters like working with people who deliver great story angles, who are easy to work with by being flexible with scheduling, and who provide great supporting materials. To add another layer on top of that, they also like working with spokespeople who can speak well during interviews, who are dynamic in their delivery, and who can provide expert commentary on a key matter.

Picture this: You're sitting down after dinner to watch the local news, and you're watching an interview with a local artist who is talking about the art fair happening this weekend. The reporter introduces him as both an artist presenting his artwork and as one of the organizers and then proceeds to ask him, "Can you tell us a little about what people can expect this week?" There's an awkward, long pause, which seamlessly transitions into an "um" before stumbling into a brief overview of "artists of all kinds coming together on Sunday, April fifth." His answer comes across as short and not thorough or detailed enough to entice anyone to come out to support the cause.

The reporter attempts to help him along by asking, "Where will the proceeds from the event go to?" The response is another high-pitched "um," and then the artist continues with "All proceeds will be donated to the local children's hospital." The reporter, now seeming as if she's pulling teeth, asks, "Will there be any special exhibits featured?" The local artist responds, "Yes, there's a special exhibit to highlight the artwork developed by the children themselves."

As a viewer, you just heard of an event that will give back to children and will celebrate their artwork. At first you were interested. However, while watching the segment, you couldn't help but feel uncomfortable for the person being interviewed.

Now put that awkward moment in the past. Instead, think of watching a national business news network on television, and the guests are speaking so quickly in tandem with the hosts that you can't help but be amazed and wonder, *How do they do that?* and better yet, *How do they know so much?* Well, those guests have been media trained and likely have done tons of other interviews. There's also a very good chance those guests have been on the show several times before, and by now, they know how to stay poised and can answer nearly any question quickly and seamlessly. Their nonverbal cues match the confidence level of their verbal messaging. They sound and look like the experts they indeed are.

When people hear the word *um* being used, they usually think it's a nervous reaction. In reality, people use ums as a way to give themselves time to complete their thought, which is usually on the spot during live interviews. *Merriam-Webster* defines *um* as being "used to indicate hesitation,"[1] and that hesitation comes from the person not knowing where they are going with their thought. Ums can be avoided by using a pause, which allows you time to breathe and think of your next statement. The pause takes up the same amount of time as the um and produces the same result, but it presents better. Ums cause you to look nervous, which translates into less confidence and diminishes your appearance as an expert.

During interviews, verbal is the most obvious form of communication, which is key to ensuring your message is clear, concise, complete, and consistent. Not only is *what* you say important; *how* you say it is. The "how" of a message is what is referred to as *paralinguistics*. The elements of paralinguistics include volume, speed, inflection, and timing, along with gestures and other nonverbal cues. If you say something too quickly, you run the risk of losing the listener, or if you raise your pitch, you risk coming across as too loud or excited. The actual content of your message gets lost when the paralinguistics don't align.

When the interview is in person, that's when you see people stumble, because it's difficult to manage the verbal message and nonverbal communication all at once. For instance, if someone is self-conscious about how they are appearing, their mind is occupied with thoughts that stem from nerves. When this happens, it's hard for their mind to recall talking points, let alone think clearly enough to deliver a good interview.

Other methods of delivering nonverbal communication include the following:

- Facial expressions

- Gestures

- Posture

- Eye gaze

- Dress

Facial Expressions

One thing to remember when doing video interviews is that whatever the camera captures will be amplified on-screen for people watching. Your facial expressions are one of the main visuals people will notice, because the camera will zoom in for close-ups as you speak. If you are nervous, your eyes will show it. Nerves are normal, and some people will always be a little nervous, regardless of how long they've been doing video interviews. However, if you consciously avoid translating that nervousness into your facial expressions, your audience may never realize just how nervous you really are. If the interview topic has a happy tone, then a natural smile is appropriate. Don't force a large smile, though. Only smile large when it's genuine.

For more serious interviews, a relaxed face is the most common approach. When not speaking, your face will be neutral, so it's important to know how you appear to others with a resting face. For some, a resting face does not translate well on television. Some may even say they have "resting bitch face," where they appear angry when they're really not. An easy way to find out how you look is by videoing yourself and watching the playback or simply asking close friends and family their opinions. The goal of a resting face is to have no tension or scowls or pursed lips, so keep your face muscles relaxed with a mildly pleasant expression.

Gestures

There are some experts who think there should be no hand movement during interviews, but I offer clients the opposite suggestion. It may make someone appear stiff and unrelatable if they don't use their hands. It can also cause the person being interviewed to become self-conscious, and I'd much rather they keep their focus on their message delivery. That being said, I do tell clients to keep their hand gestures to a minimum and below their face; this helps viewers stay focused on the person's face and words rather than the hands moving.

Another tip is to avoid putting elbows on the table in front of you or crossing your arms. This comes off as defensive and unrelatable.

A method I use to avoid appearing taut is to nod my head occasionally and when applicable. Nodding can very easily be overdone, so if you're not comfortable with this, a good rule of thumb is to not nod more in one given interview than the number of fingers you have on one hand.

Posture

The right posture will convey confidence and power to a viewer. Proper seating is one of the most difficult things to master, because what looks best on camera is an overexaggerated posture that actually feels awkward to the person doing it. When seated for an interview, you should be in the front or middle of your seat; the space from the small of your back to the back of the chair should be equivalent to the size of your fist. Don't cross your legs, unless you're crossing just at the ankles. Also, don't show the bottom of your shoe to the audience. It's distracting, and no one wants to see a dirty sole. Tighten your core with shoulder blades pulled back. I highly suggest practicing in the mirror and recording yourself to watch the playback. You want to avoid any bit of a round shoulder, since that will be magnified on camera.

Eye Gaze

One thing people often forget to keep in check is their eyes. It's an easily overlooked detail. As Allan and Barbara Pease discuss in their *Definitive Book of Body Language*, "The eyes can be the most revealing and accurate of all human communication signals."[2] Think about when you're talking to someone in person. You're face-to-face, and it's just the two of you talking. As you chat, you notice that the person's eyes are looking past you to the left, and then you follow as their gaze goes to the right. The motion alone makes you realize the person recognized someone who was walking behind you, and they're possibly paying more attention to this than to your actual conversation. Now picture watching an interview on television, and the camera is close up on the person's face. If the person being interviewed is looking at the producer walking behind the camera, you'll likely notice that as the viewer.

During TV interviews that require you to be in studio, you want to look directly at the interviewer as if it were a personal conversation. Just pretend the camera isn't there. The same goes for when a reporter comes to you with a video camera. If you are doing the interview remotely, you'll need to stare directly into the camera for it to translate well to TV and for it to seem as though you are talking directly to the host. With staring, you also have to be conscious not to become too stoic to avoid giving a deer-in-the-headlights appearance. Keep relaxed and remember to blink naturally, but don't overcompensate.

Dress

No matter who you are, you'll likely wonder about your wardrobe for the interview. You don't want to blend in to the set, and you certainly don't want to make headlines for being the "worst dressed," but what you may not realize is there are actual tips and strategies for looking your best while on camera. After all, you want viewers to focus on your face and what you say, not on your clothes.

Following are some tips for your interview:

- Softer colors are more flattering.

- The safest color on TV is blue.

- Best to avoid white, red, or black. White glows and becomes the most noticeable thing on the TV screen, while black is too harsh and can suck up all the light. Reds bleed on camera and are distracting.

- Don't wear checkers, stripes, herringbone, or small, intricate designs.

- Unless the producer explicitly tells you otherwise, avoid visible logos and company names or brands, except for your own company logo.

A confident presentation of yourself makes for a more captivating interview. By incorporating these tips, you are sure to have a more successful interview.

PREPARATION

Benjamin Franklin has been credited with saying, "By failing to prepare, you are preparing to fail." While some people may argue that this depends on the context of the situation, in terms of preparing for an interview, this statement is completely accurate. You can't just walk into an interview without having done prep work. If you do, you're leaving yourself vulnerable to potentially difficult questions that you won't know the answer to.

I help my clients prepare before an interview by starting with the interview topic that was given by the producer. From there, I have them break down their key talking points. Video interviews vary in length, but you can expect them to be between three and five minutes. That time goes by quicker than you can imagine, so realistically you aren't able to get in absolutely everything you planned for. What I suggest is to pull your three most important talking points to the top of your list. These are messages that no matter how much information you include, you absolutely want to get in. Three is a realistic number, because it allows room for the interviewer to ask their questions about each topic, and it leaves a buffer for you to work those talking points into your responses without feeling forced.

When developing your talking points, think about who the audience is and the information that would resonate most with them. Identify the three major points you hope to get across, and memorize them until they are so comfortable that the words just roll off your tongue. Some information that you may want to avoid sharing includes anything that is proprietary, anything that could be offensive or controversial, company information that has not yet been announced, and any complicated projects that require in-depth explanations, since your time is limited.

👣 Innovation Station 👣

Once you have a lead, you will want to ensure the entire process goes smoothly. From responding promptly and efficiently to the reporter to delivering the best interview you can, you want to make sure you do everything as perfectly as possible. If there are outside reasons for the media placement not coming to fruition, at least you did everything right from your end. Being a great interviewee helps ensure the reporter has enough information to write an in-depth story in print and for television. By proving you are easy to work with and can deliver good material, you demonstrate your value to the media outlet. And remember, a guest that viewers like seeing and hearing from is one that will always be welcomed back.

CHAPTER 12

Celebrate the Win

Never celebrate too early. . . . You never know what
the very next moment is going to unfold.

—JAY ARMIT, YourQuote post, January 26, 2018

Back in 2016, a local high school basketball team in Rhode Island thought they won a state title. *USA Today* reported, "The Broncos led by a point and stole the inbounds pass. That should have done it, but the Burrillville player tossed the ball backward into the air in an effort to run out the clock. The team stormed the court after the buzzer sounded, but there was still time left."[1]

While the celebration was happening, the referees ruled a player from the opposing team had possession, so their coach called time-out with one second left. With time, albeit very little, to spare and the other team too busy celebrating, the players did an alley-oop pass to one another and—low and behold—became the real winners of the Division III title.

As with every win, there's always the chance that something can go wrong. Even up until the very last second, you'll want to monitor and treat the process with the utmost care. If you allow room for an opportunity to slip through your hands, it will. In public relations, you can prevent yourself from losing the media opportunity by being as thorough as possible, beginning with following up after the interview takes place.

AFTER THE INTERVIEW

If you're working with spokespeople, it's important to find out just how the interview went. Do you need to supply the reporter with any additional information via email? Did the reporter say when the story would run? Find out if those details have already been shared, and then check in with the reporter. Ask how the interview went on their end and if they have any follow-up questions. I also recommend that you offer to assist with any next steps. In your email, you can also reconfirm your spokesperson's credit line. The format can look similar to my credit line:

> Jenna Guarneri, founder/CEO of JMG Public
> Relations and author of *You Need PR*

If the interview is for online publication, I would also include hyperlinks to the pertinent websites. For some people, their credit line can be quite lengthy, and that's great. You should be proud to share all your accolades. The problem with this, however, is that the writer likely can't include all of that within their story. Your credit line should not be longer than a sentence, and it definitely shouldn't look like a paragraph of its own. For our clients with a string of accolades, we prioritize their current position at their highest-priority company, in addition to their current accolade or project. In the example of my own credit line, my being the CEO of JMGPR is my day job, and my book, the one you're reading right now, is a prominent recent project. I may eventually swap out the author title for something else, but for now, that's a priority.

You also want to remember to humanize the interaction by thanking the reporter for their time. A little gratitude goes a long way, and it adds the human element of consideration into a conversation that is already business based. After the interview commences, it's not uncommon for reporters to ask for a follow-up call or to email back some clarifying questions. As the reporter starts to write the story and their thoughts are flowing, they may realize there's a bit of information they would like to elaborate on that they didn't ask about during the actual interview. Always submit those details back to the reporter as soon as possible.

People are always excited for a story to go live, but sometimes that eagerness turns into an annoyance for a reporter. When you send that follow-up email asking how the interview went, you can ask if the reporter has an idea of when the story may run. Some reporters will give you an exact date, and others will tell you it's out of their hands once they submit the story to their editors. In this case, it will be up to the media outlet to decide when it will run. It can be days, weeks, and sometimes even months. When this happens, it's okay to ask the reporter how long on average it takes for a submitted story to go live. If the reporter doesn't get back to you, don't follow up just yet. Reporters are busy handling interview requests one after another, so once they submit their story on you, they've already moved on to the next.

I tell people to be happy with the fact that they have a story running. It's more important to maintain the relationship with the reporter afterward, so it's not a priority to continuously reach out to that person for a response. It's okay to follow up the next week and then two weeks after that. The easiest way to find out when your story will run is to monitor the media outlet on a daily basis. Another option is to set Google alerts with your spokesperson's name and the company name so you will receive notification almost within hours of the story going live, so long as it is online.

AFTER THE STORY RUNS

Now you may be feeling congratulations are in order and it's time to celebrate. Actually, we're not quite there yet. There are a few house-keeping items you need to do before you move on from that media interview. For example, is your company name spelled properly, as well as the names of your spokespeople? Are the stats you provided accurate? Accidents happen even for reporters; they are human, after all. Because reporters are so inundated, they don't always have time to fact-check their stories before they go live, and there is the pos-sibility of an error or two occurring.

A fact check is when a reporter emails you before their story runs and asks you to confirm the information they plan to include.

This way, if there are any edits to make, they can do it before the story publishes. Fact checks happen more for print publications than online publications, since print is hard to fix after the fact. If the story is online and there are errors regarding key information, it's completely okay to politely ask for an update on those items. When I say "politely," I mean this: Start your email off by thanking the reporter for the feature, and then go into how you noticed a few errors and reference them.

One thing I don't suggest is asking them to fix slight grammatical errors that a reader may not even notice. It can come off as insulting to the reporter that someone is pointing out minor mistakes. It's better to keep these types of requests to a minimum and to include only edits on company statistics and names and factual errors.

Thank-Yous

Even when there aren't edits to be made, you should always make a habit of reaching out to a reporter after a story runs to thank them. This helps establish respect and build a good rapport for future interactions. While the reporter likely won't write a second story about you anytime soon, the goal is to continue the relationship, and perhaps down the line there will be an opportunity for something else.

I often like to send an email, since the receipt is instantaneous. Then I also send a handwritten note by mail. When someone receives something unexpectedly that is handwritten and on pretty stationery, they feel appreciated, and it can even put a smile on their face. It's an underutilized gesture that can really create an emotional and memorable response. I also make sure to add that person to our holiday mailing list. That way, even if we haven't corresponded for months, they will see my name pop up in their email. It shows I took the time to remember them and that I didn't treat the interaction like a one-off engagement. By taking these steps, I'm showing them that I'm making an effort to build a long-standing relationship with them.

Share Away

After you review your story and thank the reporter, the media-placement process is still not yet over. After the story runs, you can extend its lifespan by posting it to all social media channels, including those of the founder and team members. A thank-you in the post to the writer is always a nice way to show appreciation to the reporter. You should also tag the media outlet. This way, there's an opportunity for both the reporter and the media outlet to reshare the article to their social media channels.

If your founder is posting the article to their social media channels, they can even tag the other individuals mentioned in the post. This creates more opportunities for connections and reshares. You can also monitor who on social media shared the article to their own personal shares, then reshare their post, and thank them for it. Another option is to create sponsored content, where you put a select amount of marketing dollars into promoting the post so it comes up in more people's feeds. This will help increase views, as well as clicks back to the company website, and may even increase your social media follower count.

The sharing doesn't end there! After you did all that work to secure the media placement, you want to make sure you share it with as many people as possible. This includes distributing the story through your company newsletter, updating the company press kit with the media placement, and adding it to the "Press" section of your website. Adding an "As Seen In" on your homepage with the logos of the media outlets can also draw people's attention as soon as they come to your website. The logos can even be hyperlinked, so when someone clicks on the logo, it brings them straight to the article. You can also use quotes from the press feature for marketing materials. When you do this, the name of the publication will appear next to the quote and serve as a testimonial for potential customers.

Always remember, press begets press. Once you secure one media placement, you can share that as an update in an email with reporters from other media outlets. You can share it with anyone, except if they are a competitor of that media outlet. In this case, a competitor may say, "We won't feature a story if our competitor ran it already." This is understandable, because everyone wants to be first. If a reporter is the second one to cover a story for a media outlet with the same audience, they are late to the game and run the risk of printing "old news."

When this happens, your email can be sent outside of the normal pitch/follow-up email cycle. Perhaps you pitched someone two months ago and they never answered you. This type of email is a good way to check in with the reporter and keep them up to speed on all the buzz the company has been receiving. You want to create a sense of FOMO with reporters. Any reporter worth their salt doesn't want to miss out on a story of the next "it" brand.

Here's an example of what an update email might look like:

> Hi, [Name],
>
> I wanted to check in to update you, as we were just featured in [Media outlet name, hyperlinked]! The feature discusses _____, _____, and _____. I'd like to share a new bit of information with you that hasn't been covered anywhere else as of yet. [Share new information.] Please let me know if you think this would be of interest for future coverage.
>
> I am available for an informational call or to answer any questions you may have.
>
> Thank you, and I look forward to your feedback.
>
> Best,
> [Your name]

In addition to attracting followers and boosting your media pipeline, a media placement bolsters your reputation with current and prospective investors, customers, and employees. Having your name associated with that of a top media outlet creates instant credibility. It says a lot about a company when a reporter takes the time to write a feature story on them. Reporters look for interesting news angles and for changemakers who are offering a product or service so innovative that more people need to know about it. If a reporter has spent time interviewing a company, then a sales rep or investor will also think that company is worth closer attention. Having buzz around a company also helps with recruiting new employees. After all, who doesn't want to work for the most talked about company in the industry? The media attention creates excitement for not only your staff but potential new hires, too.

❦❦ Innovation Station ❦❦

By being thorough in your work and strategic in your approach, you can lessen the odds of your media placement falling through. Should it still happen, you know at least you did everything in your power and that all that work can still be used toward pitching another media outlet for that story. Once the story does run, you can maximize its reach by sharing it across all communication channels. I also view the media placement as an open door for continuing my relationship with that reporter. They remember your name, they know how easy you are to work with, and they know you will pitch them a great story. Securing your first media placement is just the start of your public relations journey. Once you take that first step, you'll be that much closer to becoming a PR professional yourself!

Conclusion

You may be feeling overwhelmed, or you may be so overjoyed that you've already started jotting down ideas. Whichever it may be, you can be guaranteed that you now have the knowledge to set yourself up for success as you journey on in your PR endeavors. PR can be a lot of fun, so be creative and use this time to think outside the box. Be excited about your business and share the enthusiasm. As you do, your energy will radiate, and it will create genuine connections to those listening.

ESTABLISH

As with any good idea, you need to make sure you properly plan before you execute it. PR is a lot like building a home. A secure and stable home requires a strategically crafted, interconnected system. If the team is not working off of the same blueprints or not communicating with one another about the tasks they each need to accomplish, they run the risk of building a poor-quality house with an unstable foundation. Any errors may cause your team to have to backtrack on their work or, worse, start all over.

For you today, that means starting with your brand identity and asking yourself questions like "Who am I?" and "What do I stand for?" Define your purpose, and know when the best time is for you as a brand to start the PR process. If you start pitching to the media but your messaging is weak or confusing, you run the risk of creating a poor first impression and potentially losing the opportunity for any media coverage.

Adding the human factor into your PR strategy will help create emotional connections to not only the media person but also their end reader. Emotions help stimulate memories, which means your customer will be more likely to remember and recognize your company name moving forward.

PR requires a constant flow of communication, and by creating content on a regular basis, you increase your chances of being heard by your target audience. Whether it's video, audio, or written content, you'll want to always ensure the content is meaningful and that you are providing value to your reader.

BUILD

The press kit will become one of your most important tools for pitching to the media. If the materials are too long, you'll lose the reader, and if they are too brief, then the reader will never get your point. Spend time on this and be picky about it. The press kit is your story in a nutshell. How you feel about the brand should be portrayed in it as well.

Publicists are storytellers, so get used to developing new ways to tell the same story or, better yet, come up with a brand-new one.

A good storyteller is also a good communicator; they know how to entice their listener while leaving them with the best possible perception of them and their company.

The PR process requires you to do a deep dive into not only your brand but your competitors. This will help you differentiate yourself not only in the market but also within your PR campaign. How has the media featured your competitors before? What type of media coverage did they get? Was it a large feature in a local newspaper, or was it a small mention in a national print magazine? Understanding the differences will help you understand where you fall in the mix and what you need to do to establish yourself in the market more than your competitors already have.

LAUNCH

This is where you start to see all your hard work pay off. After you've laid the groundwork, you can start planning on how you'll execute all your strategies. You can start to have fun and develop creative approaches for delivering a message, such as newsjacking a breaking news story as a short-term strategy method or using the spokesperson for their industry experience, also known as thought leadership.

You can also start to research and cultivate relationships with the media. Understanding the dynamic of the media-publicist relationship will be key to your success. Treat the pitching process with care, and respect the invisible boundaries that exist in this world. Remember, you catch more bees with honey, so treat each interaction with a media person from a place of positivity. Also, keep in mind that it's a two-way street, so make sure you are bringing the media person as much value as they would be giving you should they decide to feature you in the press. By presenting a story that appeals to their audience, you are creating a mutually beneficial relationship. When pitching a story, know how to deliver it by following the five Ws: who, what, where, when, and why. The more concise and thorough your information is, the more likely you will receive a response back from a reporter.

DELIVER

Now that you have the tools to help you *establish* who you are as a brand, you can *build* the press materials you will need to help you launch your pitching process and then *deliver* on the best possible media interview. You will then have the best possible media placement to share with the world. Figure C.1 shows a recap of the PR pitching cycle.

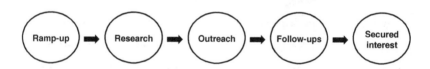

Figure C.1. The PR pitching cycle

The follow-up stages can be the most daunting for a publicist, because it can take weeks, even months, to hear back from a pitch. Sometimes you don't hear back at all. But once you sink your teeth into your first big fish, you'll be hooked! The feeling you get from a media placement after it runs can't be replaced. It's the greatest reward. Personally, we love being the ones to share the good news with our clients first so we can see their excitement. But as you now know, the work doesn't stop with the win; you must share that good press with the world and place it within your content calendar for sharing across all communication channels.

Now it's time to spread your wings and soar higher than you ever imagined possible! You believed enough in yourself to start a business, so share it with the world and allow others the opportunity to see exactly what you already know. PR gives you the chance to magnify your big, meaningful purpose, so use what you've learned from reading this book and tell the world you're here and ready to be heard.

I'm honored that you chose me to help you along your PR journey, and I'm thankful for the possibility of making even the smallest difference in your journey as an entrepreneur. For more information about *You Need PR*, visit www.youneedpr.co, or for information about JMG Public Relations, visit www.jmgpublicrelations.com.

Feel free to connect with me and share updates on your PR wins via LinkedIn or on Instagram @jenguarneri.

Acknowledgments

You very rarely get the opportunity to sit down and think about the names of every single person who has ever had an impact on your life, leading up to this very moment today. Yet here I am, realizing how hard a job this really is! The outstanding individuals I've come across during my life make me feel like one of the luckiest people on the planet. I am truly blessed to be surrounded by such inspiring and humbling people in my life.

I thank my husband, Joseph Amato, for being my biggest supporter and for always pushing me to pursue each and every win, whether at work or in my personal life. I thank him for understanding the importance of women in leadership and the need for us as individuals to fulfill our personal goals. I hope that the passion for life and curiosity of my godchildren, Ava Francesca Ferrara and Salvatore Frank Amato, stay with them forever. May they reach for the stars and be nothing short of the best versions of themselves.

Others in my family also deserve my sincere thanks. My parents, Linda and Bill Guarneri, never allowed us to settle for ordinary and taught us to always give 100 percent in everything we do. I appreciate my mom for being an extraordinary example of what a powerful woman can be. And I thank my dad for showing us that nothing in life is worth giving up on and that the fight is only half the battle. I admire my sister, Tara Guarneri, for being the first to set the bar as high as she did (no pun intended for the corporate attorney) in her career and for our family. My brother, Joseph Guarneri, shared his bravery and showed me that courage is not the absence of fear. I am grateful for Jack Guarneri, my German shepherd, second brother, and greatest friend I'll ever have, for loving each one of us unconditionally and for being the joy our family needed during some very difficult times. My grandparents, Jerry and Paca Scarpati, acted as a second set of parents to us during our childhood. Their loss has left a void in all of our hearts. I hope they look down from heaven proud of the legacy they've left behind.

Many thanks go to the incredibly talented team at JMGPR: Kathy Berardi, Cirilo Nala, Sara Lambley, Kristen Aikey, Marisa Davis, Kira Perdue, Tiara Luten, Kyla Chalmers, John Jefferson Rosales, Caressa Nala, Zel Higuit, Carli Evilsizer, Alexandra Anastasio, Aimee LaLiberte, Lisa Monaco, and Lauren Spain. I also thank all the students who have interned with us at JMGPR for being rock stars and showing up each and every day with such enthusiasm and fresh eyes to take on the world.

I am grateful to those who contributed to the making of the book: Scott Omelianuk, Chris Metinko, Joelle Garguilo, and Anna Medaris Miller, as well as the team at Greenleaf Book Group: Diana Ceres, Lindsay Bohls, Rebecca Logan, Elizabeth Brown, Kirstin Andrews, Mimi Bark, David Endris, Tiffany Barrientos, and Amanda Marquette.

Thanks go to my mentor Howard Geltzer for believing in me and for helping me understand just how much I can actually achieve. Thanks also go to the Entrepreneurs' Organization community for creating a safe space for like-minded individuals to grow and learn from one another. In addition, I thank my mentors within the Entrepreneurs' Organization Accelerator program—Brad Ginsburg, Mario Costanz, Joe Giovannoli, Danny Mizrahi, and Jeff Halevy— for challenging me on each and every occasion. I thank Juliana Barcia for understanding me like no one else does.

Space constraints don't allow me to acknowledge everyone who helped contribute in some way to who I am today. I hope they know that they are all important to me.

Notes

Introduction

1. Ivy Lee, *Mr. Lee's Publicity Book: A Citizen's Guide to Public Relations* (New York: PRMuseum Press, 2017).

Chapter 1

1. *Merriam-Webster Dictionary*, s.v. "public relations," https://www.merriam -webster.com/dictionary/public%20relations.

2. Louise Balle, "Information on Small Business Startups," *Houston Chronicle*, https://smallbusiness.chron.com/information-small-business-startups-2491 .html (accessed November 11, 2021).

3. Zendesk, "The Business Impact of Customer Service on Customer Lifetime Value," *Zendesk Blog*, April 8, 2013, https://www.zendesk.com/blog/customer -service-and-lifetime-customer-value/.

4. Center for Biological Diversity, "A Deadly Toll," https://www.biological diversity.org/programs/public_lands/energy/dirty_energy_development/oil _and_gas/gulf_oil_spill/a_deadly_toll.html (accessed November 11, 2021).

5. Gus Lubin, "BP CEO Tony Hayward Apologizes for His Idiotic Statement: 'I'd Like My Life Back,'" *Business Insider*, June 2, 2010, https://www.business insider.com/bp-ceo-tony-hayward-apologizes-for-saying-id-like-my-life -back-2010-6.

6. Joseph A. DeVito, *The Interpersonal Communication Book*, 12th ed. (Boston: Pearson, 2008).

7. Sophie Downes, "Seth Godin Wants You to Act Like a Human," *Inc.*, May 20, 2020, https://www.inc.com/sophie-downes/seth-godin-marketing-brand -crisis-pandemic.html.

8. Téa Silvestre Godfrey, "Your Brand and the Marketing Rule of 7," *Story Bistro*, October 1, 2021, http://storybistro.com/your-brand-and-the -marketing-rule-of-7/.

Chapter 2

1. Nicole Audrey, "Consumers Prefer 'Honest' Brands—and Are Willing to Pay Extra for Them," *NBC News*, September 8, 2016, https://www.nbcnews .com/business/consumer/consumers-prefer-honest-brands-are-willing-pay -extra-them-n644916.

2. Patagonia, "Core Values," https://www.patagonia.com/core-values/ (accessed October 25, 2021).

3. Poonkulali Thangavelu, "The Success of Patagonia's Marketing Strategy," *Investopedia*, February 3, 2020, https://www.investopedia.com/articles/ personal-finance/070715/success-patagonias-marketing-strategy.asp.

4. Simon Sinek, David Mean, and Peter Docker, *Find Your Why: A Practical Guide for Discovering Purpose for You and Your Team* (New York: Penguin, 2017), 16.

5. Rhett Power, "How to Humanize Your Customer Experience," *Inc.*, July 16, 2019, https://www.inc.com/rhett-power/how-to-humanize-your-customer -experience.html.

6. Larry Alton, "How to Gain Customer Appreciation—and Why You Should," *Small Business Trends*, January 16, 2018, https://smallbiztrends .com/2018/01/ways-to-show-clients-your-appreciation.html.

7. MMA, "T-Mobile: T-Mobile Tuesdays," https://www.mmaglobal.com/case -study-hub/case_studies/view/46439 (accessed October 25, 2021).

8. Ed O'Boyle, "Retail and the 'New Normal,'" Gallup, April 27, 2010, https:// news.gallup.com/businessjournal/127520/retail-new-normal.aspx.

9. O'Boyle, "Retail and the 'New Normal.'"

10. Warby Parker, "History," https://www.warbyparker.com/history (accessed October 25, 2021).

11. Lindsay Macdonald, "43 Statistics about User-Generated Content You Need to Know," *Stackla*, March 5, 2019, https://stackla.com/resources/blog/42 -statistics-about-user-generated-content-you-need-to-know/.

12. Kylie Jane Wakefield, "How Whole Foods Maintains a Healthy Twitter Strategy," *Contently*, March 14, 2012, https://contently.com/2012/03/14/ whole-foods-twitter-strategy/.

Chapter 3

1. Lyfe Marketing, "Why Is Content Marketing Important? Learn the Importance of Content Marketing for Your Business," August 4, 2020, https:// www.lyfemarketing.com/blog/why-is-content-marketing-important/.

2. HubSpot, "The Ultimate List of Marketing Statistics for 2021," https://www .hubspot.com/marketing-statistics (accessed October 25, 2021).

3. Statista, "Percentage of Internet Users Who Watch Online Video Content on Any Device as of January 2018, by Country," January 2018, https:// www.statista.com/statistics/272835/share-of-internet-users-who-watch -online-videos/.

4. Corey Ferreira, "How to Start a Successful Podcast (with under $100)," *Shopify*, February 28, 2020, https://www.shopify.com/blog/34911301-how -to-start-a-podcast-the-ultimate-step-by-step-podcasting-guide.

5. Pamela Bump, "31 LinkedIn Stats That Marketers Need to Know in 2021," *HubSpot*, March 22, 2021, https://blog.hubspot.com/marketing/linkedin-stats.

6. Kylee Lessard, "The 11 Best Small Business LinkedIn Pages We've Seen," *LinkedIn Marketing Blog*, January 1, 2020, https://www.linkedin.com/ business/marketing/blog/linkedin-pages/the-11-best-small-business-linkedin -pages-we-ve-ever-seen.

7. Sean Callahan, "7 Examples of Powerful Thought Leadership on LinkedIn," *LinkedIn Marketing Blog*, December 30, 2020, https://www.linkedin.com/business/marketing/blog/content-marketing/7-examples-of-powerful-thought-leadership-on-linkedin.

8. Aaron Smith and Monica Anderson, "Social Media Use in 2018," Pew Research Center, March 1, 2018, https://www.pewresearch.org/internet/2018/03/01/social-media-use-in-2018/.

Chapter 4

1. Founder Institute, "Startup Madlibs: Perfecting Your One Sentence Pitch," https://fi.co/madlibs (accessed October 25, 2021).

2. "Orangetheory Fitness Supports the #FreeBritney Movement," *PR Newswire*, August 13, 2021, https://www.prnewswire.com/news-releases/orangetheory-fitness-supports-the-freebritney-movement-301355060.html.

Chapter 5

1. Grace Miller, "42 Referral Marketing Statistics That Will Make You Want to Start a RAF Program Tomorrow," Annex Cloud, https://www.annexcloud.com/blog/42-referral-marketing-statistics-that-will-make-you-want-to-start-a-raf-program-tomorrow/ (accessed October 25, 2021).

2. Abstrakt Marketing Group, "From Monotone to Moving: The Power of Voice Inflection," https://www.abstraktmg.com/driving-leads/from-monotone-to-moving-the-power-of-voice-inflection/ (accessed October 25, 2021).

3. Nagesh Belludi, "Albert Mehrabian's 7-38-55 Rule of Personal Communication," *Right Attitudes*, October 4, 2008, https://www.rightattitudes.com/2008/10/04/7-38-55-rule-personal-communication/.

4. Ariel Schwartz, "Toms Shoes CEO Blake Mycoskie on Social Entrepreneurship, Telling Stories, and His New Book," *Fast Company*, September 6, 2011, https://www.fastcompany.com/1678486/toms-shoes-ceo-blake-mycoskie-on-social-entrepreneurship-telling-stories-and-his-new-book.

Chapter 6

1. Joelle Garguilo, phone interview by the author, October 1, 2021.

Chapter 7

1. David Moye, "Cheerios' Tasteless Prince Tribute Bombs on Twitter," *Huff-Post*, April 21, 2016, https://www.huffpost.com/entry/cheerios-prince_n_57 193778e4b0d4d3f722c4fd.

Chapter 8

1. Chris Metinko, email correspondence with the author, August 4, 2021.

Chapter 9

1. Scott Omelianuk, Zoom interview by the author, July 9, 2021.

Chapter 10

1. Anna Medaris Miller, "Pitch Perfect Workshop with the New York Writing Room," Zoom workshop, May 12, 2021.

2. Taylor Lorenz, "Your Success Is Not a Story," *Taylor Lorenz's Newsletter*, June 8, 2020, https://taylorlorenz.substack.com/p/your-success-is-not-a-story.

Chapter 11

1. *Merriam-Webster Dictionary*, s.v. "um," https://www.merriam-webster.com/dictionary/um.

2. Christina Hennessy, "Body Language: Tips for Your TV Interview," *Through-line* (blog), April 2, 2019, https://www.throughlinegroup.com/2019/04/02/body-language-tips-for-your-tv-interview/.

Chapter 12

1. "Rhode Island Team Celebrates State Basketball Title but Ended Up Losing in Last Second," *USA Today*, February 29, 2016, https://usatodayhss.com/2016/rhode-island-team-celebrates-state-basketball-title-that-it-ended-up-losing-in-last-second.

Glossary

Advertorial: A story paid for by you, the company, that is featured as an editorial, a written piece within a media outlet.

Angle: The viewpoint of the story being pitched.

Backlink: A hyperlink in an online story that usually goes back to your company website.

Beat: The specific topics a reporter covers.

Boilerplate: A paragraph summary about your company used at the end of a press release.

Byline: An article written in the first person that's usually about a trend or specific topic.

Circulation: The total number of print copies sold by a publication in a given period of time.

Digital PR: A PR strategy specific to online media outlets, as well as social media.

Earned media: Media placements that are not paid for but are earned through the media.

Embargo: A request or requirement that a story not be released until a certain date.

Exclusive: An offering for a specific person and media outlet to cover the news first and before any other media outlet has the opportunity to do so.

Feature story: A longer story containing details and descriptors within a media outlet, also known as a *feature*.

Launch date: The official day set for an announcement to be made.

Lead time: The amount of time between pitching a media outlet and the date the media placement runs.

Media coverage: A story as it appears in the media, also known as a *media feature*.

Pay for play: When you have to pay to receive editorial coverage within a media outlet.

Pitch: The story you propose to a reporter for media coverage.

Press clip: A snapshot image of a media placement. Traditionally, the press clip was a cut out of a newspaper or magazine. Today, the term is used to describe digital files of the media placement.

Press hit: A secured media placement.

Press kit: A compilation of promotional material given to the media as a briefing about the company or person. Can also be referred to as a *media kit*.

Press tour: When company executives or individuals meet with media in a few different locations or cities to discuss a specific event or initiative that is newsworthy.

Publicist: A person responsible for promoting a company or individual.

Roundup: A media hit that is a compilation of a few different products or companies that features high-level descriptions for each.

Thought leadership: The sharing of expert knowledge by an individual on a niche topic to a larger audience.

Trade publication: A media outlet that covers a specific industry or niche.

Traditional PR: A press strategy that targets print publications as well as television and radio.

UVM (unique visitors per month): The number a media outlet uses to represent their online readership within a given month. This number represents the number of individuals who visit a website at least once within that time frame.

Wire service: A news agency that you pay to upload a press release to so it is syndicated to their distribution lists, which consist of newspapers, radio, and television stations.

Index

About the Author

JENNA GUARNERI is the chief executive officer of JMG Public Relations, an award-winning PR firm based in New York City. Jenna counsels innovators who are changing the world with their B2B and B2C venture-backed startup companies. She is known for delivering quality work while fostering meaningful relationships with her clients, team, and media contacts. Jenna is an authority with a proven track record on reputation management, media relations, and brand communication.

Before starting her own firm, Jenna worked on top-named luxury accessory and lifestyle brands and with world-renowned health and wellness experts, including the founder of an international spirits brand.

Jenna launched JMG Public Relations in 2015 to offer a unique blend of creative thinking, strategizing, and implementing public relations campaigns. Jenna and the JMG team are committed to fostering relationships that provide quality work to help clients reach a multi-platform audience while building and establishing their brands. Jenna is at the cusp of the ever-changing media world and delivers a fresh approach with high-impact results.

Serving as a communications chair for the Entrepreneurs' Organization Accelerator program in New York, Jenna is also a board member of the Pace University Transformative Leadership Certificate Program. Jenna is an adjunct professor of public relations at the Manhattan campus of St. John's University and is a regular columnist for the Forbes Business Council.

**Learn more at www.jmgpublicrelations.com
and www.youneedpr.co.**

CPSIA information can be obtained
at www.ICGtesting.com
Printed in the USA
LVHW100943200622
721657LV00003B/29